GU
G

ALA

Fodor's Travel Publications New York Toronto London Sydney Auckland

www.fodors.com

GULF COAST GETAWAYS

Editor: Diane Mehta

Production Editor: Linda K. Schmidt
Editorial Contributors: Matthew Windsor, Linda Peal, David Downing, Pamela Wiesen
Maps: David Lindroth, *cartographer*; Bob Blake and Rebecca Baer, *map editors*
Design: Bob Bull
Production/Manufacturing: Robert B. Shields
Cover Photo (St. Joseph State Park): VISIT FLORIDA

COPYRIGHT

First Edition

ISBN 1–4000–1423–9

ISSN 1548–7539

SPECIAL SALES

This book is available for special discounts for bulk purchases for sales promotions or premiums. Special editions, including personalized covers, excerpts of existing books, and corporate imprints, can be created in large quantities for special needs. For more information, write to Special Markets/Premium Sales, 1745 Broadway, MD 6-2, New York, New York 10019, or e-mail specialmarkets@randomhouse.com. Inquiries from Canada should be directed to your local Canadian bookseller or sent to Random House of Canada, Ltd., Marketing Department, 2775 Matheson Boulevard East, Mississauga, Ontario L4W 4P7. Inquiries from the United Kingdom should be sent to Fodor's Travel Publications, 20 Vauxhall Bridge Road, London SW1V 2SA, England.

A TIP & AN INVITATION

Although all prices, opening times, and other details in this book are based on information supplied to us at press time, changes occur all the time in the travel world, and Fodor's cannot accept responsibility for facts that become outdated or for inadvertent errors or omissions. So **always confirm information when it matters,** especially if you're making a detour to visit a specific place. Your experiences—positive and negative—matter to us. If we have missed or misstated something, **please write to us.** We follow up on all suggestions. Contact the Gulf Coast Getaways editor at editors@fodors.com or c/o Fodor's, 1745 Broadway, New York, NY 10019.

PRINTED IN THE UNITED STATES OF AMERICA

10 9 8 7 6 5 4 3 2

CONTENTS

GULF COAST GETAWAYS

You may call this part of the Gulf of Mexico shoreline the Redneck Riviera (the local nickname), or you may call it simply the Gulf Coast. Either way, it's one heck of a Riviera. Think white-sand beaches soft as biscuit flour, clear blue waters, native wildlife, unspoiled wilderness, and fishing villages. Until now, it's been a secret and peerless getaway close to home, a region foolishly overlooked by vacationers from farther afield seeking an escape. The Florida Panhandle alone has some of the top beaches in the country—Grayton Beach State Park, St. George Island, and St. Joe Peninsula State Park, for example. But Alabama and Mississippi have enough fine beaches to steal their share of the Sunshine State's thunder. Alabama's gems are the spectacular Gulf Shores, sitting like the dot at the end of the exclamation formed by State Road 59, and Dauphin Island, whose gleaming sands buffer Mobile Bay from storms that roar up the Gulf of Mexico. Farther west, still, on the Mississippi coast, you'll come to dynamic places like Biloxi, where the same natural environs that draw beachgoers in search of relaxation lure anglers in search of the catch of the day.

Beauty & the Beach

All along the Gulf Coast beauty abounds, but until you've seen the coastline with your own eyes, you're bound to underestimate how striking the dunes are, how Caribbean-clear the water is, and what a wonder it is that this coast hasn't been transformed into one uninterrupted Fort Lauderdale or Daytona Beach.

The secret is quickly getting out, however, a fact evidenced by the perpetual widening project of U.S. 98, the main coastal artery that runs from Alabama all the way through Florida. (Beware: traffic can come to a rush-hour standstill in areas where two lanes have yet to be widened to four.) Another example of the Gulf Coast's growing cachet is that the area recently got its first "boutique" hotel—done up in washed-out blues and seashell tones, with self-conscious architecture, expensive bed linens, and private outdoor showers. Others are bound to follow.

Seaside, Florida, a planned community of Victorian-style ginger-bread houses with picket fences and tin-roofs, made it through its first 20 years intact and today looks almost as if it actually belongs in the area. But the slow pace of life that prevails in these parts—and the tendency to take a while to warm up to change of any kind—is good news for preservation. To keep outsiders from ex-ploiting the area's natural beauty—in one local's opinion, the area is in danger of being "loved to death"—Gulf Coasters have taken to a kind of grass-roots environmentalism, brought to life by a growing awareness of the fragile relationship between nature and development. It's a scenario that's echoed offshore in the Gulf of Mexico, too, where some of the country's largest oil deposits lie at the bottom of some of the most productive fishing waters in the world. It's a balancing act, and smart local visitor bureaus and chambers of commerce are taking the lead in developing low-im-pact, sustainable tourism that can promote the area without sell-ing it out.

"A Quaint Drinking Village with a Fishing Problem"

The other good news is that the offbeat frontier mentality for which the Gulf Coast is famous shows no signs of going city-slicker. Case in point? Carrabelle, Florida, only half-jokingly known as the "quaint drinking village with a fishing problem" and once home to the World's Smallest Police Station (a phone booth off U.S. 98). Its charm remains intact, as does its humor: a popular local bumper sticker proudly asks, "Where in the Hell is Carrabelle?" Then there's lovely Apalachicola, where John Gorrie, the father of refrigeration and air-conditioning, perfected his inventions in the heat of the Gulf Coast. Apalachicola is a place of oyster boats and extra-wide brick-paved streets, a holdover from the days when bales of cotton awaiting shipment were stacked along the curbs. Before cotton and oysters were king, the town was famous for being the Gulf's sea sponge capitol, but the sponge colonies eventually died off—not from over-harvesting, goes the local joke, but rather from pure boredom.

Quirkiness prevails all along the coast. You can almost see this playful spirit flying between Alabama and Florida at the Interstate Mullet Toss, a curious fish-throwing competition held at the Flori-Bama Lounge on Florida's Perdido Key, an island between Pensacola and Alabama. At the end of April more than a thousand people pay $15 each to see who can throw a one-and-a-half-pound mullet the farthest between states. Why? Because the mullet is the only fish with a gizzard and, therefore, is believed by locals to possess mystical qualities. For a more sober look at life on the coast, head over during Christmas to Biloxi, Mississippi, for the annual Blessing of the Fleet, where the procession of shrimp boats attests to the importance the area's natural bounty plays in the lives of its many residents.

Fortified with History

The Gulf Coast is a land of historical distinctions, too. Florida's Fort Walton Beach, once a sleepy, almost uninhabited stretch of Gulf front is now home to Eglin Air Force Base, the largest single military installation in the Western Hemisphere: at 724 square mi, it's about the size of the entire state of Rhode Island. At Pensacola Beach, which anchors the eastern end of the Florida Gulf Coast, you'll find Fort Pickens, a Civil War–era fortification where portraits of its most famous detainee, Geronimo, are for sale in the gift shop. And then there's Pensacola itself, the City of Five Flags, whose dynamic blend of French, Spanish, and Georgian architecture, found in the historic districts of Seville and Palafox, proves that the area was considered worth fighting for long before the first developer ever laid eyes on it.

But the greatest assets of the Gulf Coast are timeless: the brilliant sunsets, the soothing warm waters topped with a meringue of sea foam, and the sea oats swaying in gentle Gulf breezes, as if they can't decide whether to sun on the dunes or take a dip. The natural wonders extend from Wakulla Springs and the Suwannee River across to the Gulf Islands National Seashore, which spans nearly 200 mi of barrier islands that dot the Gulf Coast. It's a getaway destination unlike any other in the country. But then, to all of us who know the Gulf Coast and love it, that's old news.

– David Downing

ABOUT THIS BOOK

There's no doubt that the best source for travel advice is a like-minded friend who's just been where you're headed. But with or without that friend, you'll have a better trip with a Fodor's guide in hand. Once you know how we rate things, you'll be in great shape to find your way around wherever it is you're going.

SELECTION Our goal is to cover the best properties, sights, and activities in their category, as well as the most interesting communities to visit. It goes without saying that no property mentioned in the book has paid to be included.

RATINGS Stars enclosed in circles denote sights and properties that our editors and writers consider the very best. These are listed below in the **Pure Gulf** section.

BUDGET WELL The approximate ranges of hotel and restaurant prices are listed at the end of each review, before the address. Hotel prices are for a standard double room in high season (typically summer, though for some places it's football season), followed by the price of suites. Restaurant prices are for a main course. For attractions, we always give standard adult admission fees. **AE, D, DC, MC, V** following restaurant and hotel listings indicate whether American Express, Discover, Diners Club, MasterCard, or Visa are accepted.

DON'T FORGET RESTAURANTS are open for lunch and dinner daily unless we state otherwise; we mention dress only when there's a specific requirement and reservations only when they're essential or not accepted—it's always best to book ahead. **Hotels** have private baths, phone, TVs, and air-conditioning and operate on the European Plan (a.k.a. EP, meaning without meals), unless we specify otherwise.

OUR CONTRIBUTORS

There's no substitute for travel advice from a good friend who knows your style, but our contributors are the next best thing—the kind of people you would poll for travel advice if you could.

Florida-raised **David Downing,** a full-time Fodor's staffer and travel columnist, has covered the Florida Panhandle for several editions of Fodor's Florida and served as editor of Compass American Guides: Florida. His writing has appeared on Fodors. com and on The New York Times online, and he's been featured as a travel expert on the Travel Channel, CNN, and numerous syndicated and local TV and radio stations across the country.

Linda Peal is a freelance writer and editor living in Oxford, Mississippi. She writes travel and literary reviews for regional publications. She also works for the University of Mississippi Chancellor as his speechwriter, and enjoys travel, literature, music, and her three children.

Pamela Wiesen has been freelancing for Fodor's Travel Guides for more than a dozen years, contributing most recently to the 12th edition of the *Official Guide to America's National Parks.* Her travels to Mississippi's Gulf Coast have given her an appreciation for the natives' friendliness, not to mention a winter climate a bit more hospitable than that of her home in Wisconsin.

A connoisseur of small towns and fine beaches, **Matthew Windsor,** a Florida transplant, has found a lot to love about Alabama and its oft-maligned Gulf Coast. He lives in Birmingham, where he contributes to several travel publications and drives the state's back roads in his spare time.

PURE GULF

Everyone's idea of fun varies. One person likes to laze around on the beach while another enjoys nothing more than a strenuous hike through a forest. Similarly, while one person loves a cozy bed-and-breakfast, another prefers a rollicking casino-hotel. That's why the following list runs the gamut of what our editors and writers consider *Pure Gulf*—the best of what the coast has to offer.

ALABAMA

SEE & DO

Bellingrath Gardens and Home, Theodore (near Mobile)
Bragg-Mitchell Mansion, Mobile
Claude Kelley State Park, Atmore
Estuarium, Dauphin Island
Fort Gaines, Dauphin Island
Gulf State Park, Gulf Shores
Old Courthouse Museum, Monroeville
U.S.S. *Alabama,* Mobile

EAT

Bayside Grill, Orange Beach
The Fairhope Inn and Restaurant, Fairhope
Gerlach's, Atmore
Justine's at the Pillars, Mobile
Loretta's, Mobile
The Outrigger, Orange Beach
Pelican Pub & Grill, Dauphin Island
Wash House, Fairhope

SLEEP

Adam's Mark Mobile, Mobile
Bay Breeze Bed & Breakfast, Fairhope

Gulf State Park Resort Hotel, Gulf Shores
Island House Hotel, Orange Beach
Malaga Inn, Mobile
Marriott's Grand Hotel Resort, Golf Club and Spa, Fairhope
Towle House, Mobile

FLORIDA

SEE & DO

Alfred Maclay Gardens State Park, Tallahassee
Blackwater River State Forest, Crestview
Blackwater River State Park, Pensacola
Downtown Tallahassee Historic Trail
Edward Ball Wakulla Springs State Park, Tallahassee
Falling Waters State Recreation Area, Chipley
Florida Caverns State Park, Marianna
Forest Capital State Museum and Cracker Homestead,
    Perry
Fort Barrancas, Pensacola
Grayton Beach State Park, Grayton Beach
Gulf Islands National Seashore, Pensacola Beach
Historic Pensacola Village, Pensacola
Howl at the Moon beachfront bar, Fort Walton
Lafayette Blue Springs, Perry
Museum of Florida History, Tallahassee
Ponce de León Springs State Recreation Area, De Funiak
    Springs
Shell Island boat trips, Panama City Beach
Silver Sands Factory Stores, Destin
St. Andrews State Park, Panama City Beach
St. George Island State Park
St. Joseph Peninsula State Park, Apalachicola
St. Joseph Peninsula State Park, St. Joseph Peninsula
St. Marks National Wildlife Refuge, Tallahassee
The Zoo, Gulf Breeze

EAT

Andrew's 228, Tallahassee
Blue Parrot, St. George Island
Cafe Thirty-A, Seaside
Criollas, Grayton Beach
Dharma Blue, Pensacola
Downtown Café of Perry
Elephant Walk, Destin
Flounder's Chowder and Ale House, Pensacola Beach
Hopkins' Eatery, Tallahassee
Jubilee, Pensacola Beach
Marina Café
Picolo Restaurant & Red Bar, Grayton Beach
Rice-Bowl Oriental, Tallahassee
Tamara's Cafe Floridita, Apalachicola
Toucan's, St. Joseph Peninsula
The Tree Steak House, Tallahassee
Red Canyon Grill, Marianna
Schooner's, Panama City Beach

SLEEP

Best Western Resort, Pensacola Beach
Comfort Inn, Pensacola Beach
The Consulate, Apalachicola
Crowne Plaza–Pensacola Grand Hotel, Pensacola
Edgewater Beach Resort, Panama City Beach
Gibson Inn, Apalachicola
Governors Inn, Tallahassee
Hilton Sandestin, Destin
Hinson House B&B, Marianna
Hotel De Funiak, De Funiak Springs
Marriott's Bay Point Resort Village, Panama City Beach
Old Salt Works Cabins, St. Joseph Peninsula
Pandora's Steakhouse and Lounge, Fort Walton
Pensacola Victorian, Pensacola

Radisson Beach Resort, Fort Walton
Sandestin Golf and Beach Resort, Destin
Seaside Cottage Rental Agency, Seaside
The St. George Inn, St. George Island
Wakulla Springs Lodge and Conference Center, Tallahassee
WaterColor Inn, Seaside

MISSISSIPPI

SEE & DO

Beauvoir, Jefferson Davis Home & Presidential Library, Biloxi
The Friendship Oak, Pass Christian
Gulf Islands National Seashore, Gulfport
Mississippi Sandhill Crane National Wildlife Refuge, Ocean
    Springs
NASA StennisSphere Space Center, Waveland
The Ohr/O'Keefe Museum of Art, Biloxi
Shearwater Pottery and Showroom, Ocean Springs
Ship Island Excursions, Gulfport
Tullis-Toledano Manor, Biloxi
Walter Anderson Museum of Art, Ocean Springs
Historic Downtown Walking Tour of Old Bay St. Louis,
    Waveland

EAT

Chappy's, Gulfport
The Chimneys, Gulfport
Jocelyn's, Ocean Springs
Lil Ray's, Bay St. Louis
Mary Mahoney's Old French House Restaurant, Biloxi
Vrazel's Fine Food, Gulfport

SLEEP

Beau Rivage, Biloxi
Father Ryan House, Biloxi
Grand Casino Gulfport Hotel & Oasis Resort and Spa, Gulfport

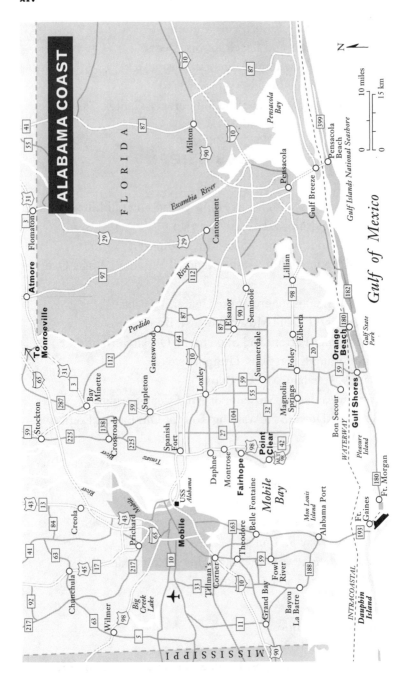

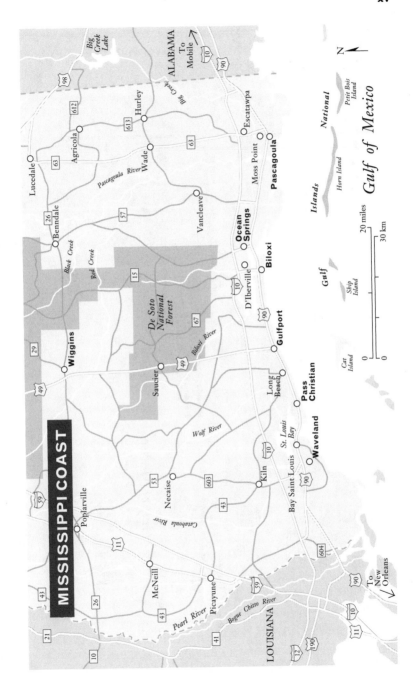

MISSISSIPPI COAST

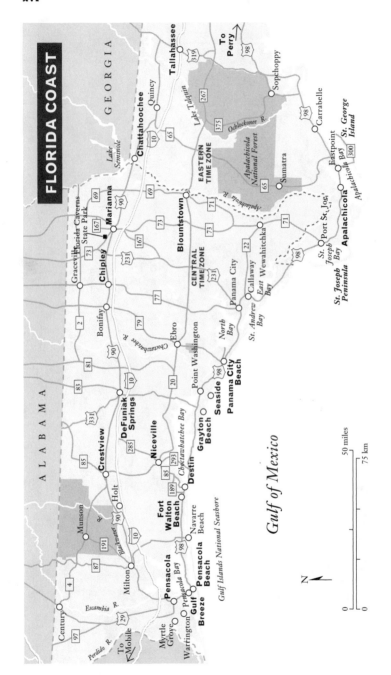

FLORIDA COAST

ATMORE

Founded in 1866 as a supply stop along the Mobile & Great Northern railroad, the city was a thriving sawmill town that was first named Williams Station. It was renamed Atmore in 1897 in honor of Charles Pawson Atmore, the general ticket agent for the Louisville & Nashville railroad. The city retains a small-town, rural style of living. Area highlights include the Poarch Creek Indian Reservation and the Claude D. Kelley State Park.

SEE & DO

✪ **CLAUDE D. KELLEY STATE PARK** This state park has a large lake for fishing and swimming, camp sites, picnic and play areas, vacation cottages, and hiking trails. It has one family cottage and a group pavilion popular for family reunions. *580 H. Kyle Rd., 36502, tel. 251/862–2511, fax 251/862–2511. $1. Daily 7–dusk.*

CREEK BINGO PALACE ♦ The Poarch Creek Native Americans are part of the original Creek Nation, and have lived together for nearly 150 years. The Poarch Creek Tribe is the only federally recognized tribe in the state of Alabama. The Palace is a high-stakes bingo casino. *Hwy. 21 S at Poarch Rd., 36502, tel. 251/368–8007 or 800/826–9121. www.creekbingo.com. $5 for bingo. Sun.–Thurs. 10–midnight, Fri. and Sat. 10–4 AM.*

WILLIAMS STATION DAY ♦ A regional festival in October, with fine arts and crafts, entertainment, logging demonstrations, food, and train displays, celebrates Atmore's railroad and sawmill heritage. *Tel. 251/368–3305.*

EAT

✪ **GERLACH'S** Built in 1930, this downtown Atmore restaurant is one of the fancier places in town. Inside the two-story building are huge bay windows, exposed brick walls, tiled floors, bouquets of fresh flowers, and linen tablecloths. Try the "citified" green tomatoes over smoked gouda grits with shrimp sauce, Gerlach's Crab Cakes with piquant sauce, or the fillet grouper pecan with Creole butter sauce. The most popular desserts are chocolate sin cake and the homemade cheesecake with raspberry and mango sauce. *$9–$20. 122 S. Main St., 36502, tel. 251/368–2433. AE, D, DC, MC, V.*

SLEEP

COMFORT INN ♦ This standard two-story hotel is off I–65, at Exit 96—if you're going south it's by the service road, and if you're going north, take the exit, go left over the interstate, then left again, into the hotel. It's also near several restaurants, including the Black Angus next door. *$60–$80. 198 Ted Bates Rd., Evergreen 36401, tel. 251/578–4701, fax 251/578–3180, www.comfortinn.com. 60 rooms. Microwaves, refrigerators, cable TV, pool, business services, some pets allowed (fee). AE, D, DC, MC, V.*

DAYS INN ♦ Just off I–65, this motel is within walking distance—right down the street—from several fast-food restaurants. If you're driving north from Mobile, take Exit 96 and turn left; if you're driving south from Montgomery, take Exit 96 and turn right. *$49;*

$59 suites. Rte. 2 (Box 389), Evergreen 36401, tel. 251/578–2100, fax 251/578–2100, www.daysinn.com. 40 rooms; 4 suites. Complimentary Continental breakfast, cable TV, some pets allowed (fee), no-smoking rooms. AE, D, DC, MC, V.

ROYAL OAKS BED & BREAKFAST ♦ This old French country–style house has a wraparound porch and is surrounded by cotton and soybean fields, vast lawns, an English garden, fruit trees, free-roaming peacocks, guineas, ducks, geese, and chickens. Inside are cathedral ceilings, king-size beds, private or shared baths, and an eclectic mix of antiques and artwork from the area and the owners' frequent trips to England. It's 5 mi north of Atmore and 6 mi from the Florida state line. A lavish full southern breakfast of bacon, eggs, grits, and fruit is included. *$75. 5415 Hwy. 21 N, 36502, tel. 251/368–8722. www.royal-oaks.homepage.com. 2 rooms. Complimentary breakfast, pool. AE, D, DC, MC, V.*

MORE INFO

ATMORE AREA CHAMBER OF COMMERCE ♦ *501 S. Pensacola Ave., Atmore 36502, tel. 251/368–3305, fax 251/368–0800. www.frontiernet. net/~atmoreal.*

GETTING HERE

Take I–65 to Exit 57 (it's the same exit from either direction), then follow AL 21 S into town.

DAUPHIN ISLAND

Three miles off the coast of Mobile County's mainland, Dauphin Island is a cigar-shape, 14-mi-long island that is less than 2 mi across at its widest point. The island has no traffic lights, four churches, several fish markets, a handful of shops, and locals accustomed to buying shrimp and flounder fresh directly from fishing boats. You can reach the island by a causeway from the mainland or by ferry at Fort Morgan Peninsula every 90 minutes from 8 AM to 5 PM.

The first European settlement in the Louisiana Territory was established on Dauphin Island by the French in the 1700s. The settlers called it "Massacre" for the large number of skeletons they found here.

Fort Gaines, which is on Dauphin Island, and its across-bay sister, Fort Morgan, were seized by Alabama troops at the start of the Civil War and became Confederate strongholds. The Mobile Bay Ferry connects Dauphin Island and Fort Morgan. A $4 million Estuarium at the Dauphin Island Sea Lab opened in 1998, spotlighting the unique local ecosystems of the Mobile Bay estuary.

SEE & DO

ALABAMA DEEP SEA FISHING RODEO ◆ Some 3,000 anglers take part in this Gulf waters fishing competition in July, and vie for thousands of dollars in cash and prizes. *Tel. 251/471–0025.*

✪ **ESTUARIUM** At the Dauphin Island Sea Lab, the Estuarium spotlights the unique local ecosystems of the Mobile Bay estuary. A Living Marsh Boardwalk includes interpretive signs explaining the natural history of the state's marshes, geography, and evolution of the barrier islands. There are displays, interactive exhibits, a 9,000-gallon aquarium simulating the brackish underwater environment of the Mobile Delta, a 16,000-gallon tank with sea life from the Gulf of Mexico, and exhibits explaining the fragile environment of the coast's barrier islands. Twenty small aquariums focus on individual species. *101 Bienville Blvd., 36528, tel. 251/861–7500, fax 251/861–4646, estuarium.disl.org. $6. Mar.–Aug., Mon.–Sat. 9–6, Sun. noon–6; Sept.–Feb., Mon.–Sat. 9–5, Sun. 1–5.*

FALL BIRD FESTIVAL ◆ Dauphin Island is a stopping point for tropical birds during the fall migration (in October) to the Yucatan. During the season there are more than 200 varieties of birds staying on this tiny island. The ornithological association on the island brings in specialists to talk about this phenomena, and there are field trips on weekends. *Tel. 251/861–2120. $15.*

✪ **FORT GAINES** The pre–Civil War fort was the setting for the famous Battle of Mobile Bay when the Union's Admiral Farragut, who would not be deterred, bellowed, "Damn the torpedoes; Full speed ahead!" and won the battle. You can touch cannons used in battle, explore tunnels and bastions, and visit a blacksmith shop, kitchen, and bakery. Living-history events are staged on selected weekends. *51 Bienville Blvd., 36528, tel. 251/861–6992, www. dauphinisland.org/fort.htm. $5. Daily 9–5.*

MOBILE BAY FERRY ♦ The ferry, which accommodates cars, RVs, and sightseers, shuttles daily between Fort Morgan and Dauphin Island. *Tel. 251/540–7787, www.mobilebayferry.com. $25 round-trip for cars, $10 one-way for cars, $5 for passengers on foot. Call for hrs.*

SPRING FESTIVAL ♦ This May event includes family events, a pier-fishing rodeo, beach run, tennis and volleyball tournaments, and a family carnival. *Dauphin Island, tel. 251/861–5524.*

EAT

✪ PELICAN PUB & GRILL This restaurant and bar in Aloe Bay was built and raised on pilings, which cut through the restaurant and give the dining room a unique layout. The current owners have replaced the rustic murals of shrimp buoys and pelicans with a more generic island motif, and have pared down the menu. The restaurant now serves mainly seafood, cheesesteaks, and New Orleans–style po'boys. Dine outdoors either up or downstairs: both locations look out onto the bay. *$10–$20. 1102 Desoto Ave., 36528, tel. 251/861–7180. AE, MC, V.*

SLEEP

BAYSIDE MOTEL ♦ This small, simple motel in Indian Bay is predominantly used by fishing enthusiasts. The building is surrounded by fishing docks and boat slips. The motel coffee shop only serves lunch. The one luxury offered here is a view of Indian Bay from every window. The closest swimming beach is 3 mi away. *$54. 510 Lemoyne Dr., 36528, tel. 251/861–4994. 23 rooms. Restaurant, coffee shop, microwaves, refrigerators, cable TV; no room phones. AE, D, MC, V.*

GULF BREEZE MOTEL ♦ This family-owned motel has spacious rooms and two-bedroom efficiencies with fully equipped kitchens. It's near the public beach and a boat launch on the bay side of the island. *$49–$59; $69–$79 apartments. 1512 Cadillac Ave., 36528, tel. 251/861–7344 or 800/286–0296, www.gulfinfo.com/gulfbreezemotel. 25 rooms; 6 apartments. Refrigerators, cable TV, some pets allowed (fee). AE, D, MC, V.*

HARBOR LIGHTS INN ♦ This small island inn is within walking distance of the public beach and offers two-bedroom suites and a view of Mobile Bay. *$79. 1506 Cadillac Ave., 36528, tel. 251/861–7344 or 800/286–0296, www.gulfinfo.com/gulfbreezemotel. 7 suites. Kitchenettes, cable TV, dock, fishing. AE, D, MC, V.*

MORE INFO

TOWN OF DAUPHIN ISLAND TOWN HALL ♦ *Bienville Blvd. (Box 610), Dauphin Island 36528, tel. 251/861–5525, www.townofdauphinisland. org.*

GETTING HERE

The quickest and easiest way to reach Dauphin Island is via the causeway-bridge from the mainland. Turn off I–10 at Exit 17 onto AL 193 S. Another option is the Mobile Bay Ferry from Fort Morgan, which makes the 45-minute trip daily from 8 AM to 5 PM.

FAIRHOPE & POINT CLEAR

Clinging to the eastern shore of Mobile Bay, the quiet towns of Fairhope and Point Clear have restored clapboard houses with wide porches overlooking the bay and live oak trees cloaked with Spanish moss.

Fairhope was settled around 1900 by a group of Midwesterners, who established it as a utopian single-tax community (the system is still in use). Today Fairhope's streets are lined with seasonal flowers year-round—even the trash receptacles double as planters—and the downtown area has antiques shops, funky stores, art galleries, and B&Bs, making it a relaxing weekend escape. The Fairhope Municipal Pier, the centerpiece of town, offers fishing, boating, and marine services. Fairhope's Arts and Crafts Festival, held each March, is a large juried show that draws more than 200 exhibitors for a weekend.

Point Clear's incomparable Grand Hotel, operating since 1847, is a leading resort destination hidden away among million-dollar bayside estates. A walk along the hotel's boardwalk provides a glimpse of the summer homes that line Mobile Bay.

SEE & DO

FAIRHOPE ARTS AND CRAFTS FESTIVAL ♦ Held on the third weekend of March, this three-day celebration is the town's largest event of the year. Main streets close down and some 250 arts-and-crafts booths line the streets. For entertainment, there's everything from high school bands to local musicians, gymnasts, and dance performances. Street vendors from the local restaurants sell food, and there are also rides and a children's train that circumnavigates the streets. *Tel. 251/928–6387 or 251/621–8222.*

RIVIERA CENTRE ♦ This sprawling shopping paradise of more than 120 factory outlet stores is 15 mi south of Fairhope. *2601 S. Mackenzie St., Foley 36535, tel. 251/943–8888. www.shoprivieracentre. com. Mon.–Sat. 10–9, Sun. 11–6.*

EAT

✪ THE FAIRHOPE INN AND RESTAURANT Owner-chef Tyler Kean's restaurant, inside a B&B, is fast becoming "the" place to dine in Fairhope. The small, elegant dining room extends onto an enclosed porch that overlooks a lush private courtyard. Kean's menu changes seasonally but may include pan-roasted grouper with asparagus and morel mushrooms in a red-wine sauce served over grits. Sunday brunch is quite popular. *$17–$25. 63 S. Church St., Fairhope 36532, tel. 251/928–6226. AE, D, DC, MC, V. Closed Mon.*

PINK PELICAN AT THE POINTE ♦ With views of Mobile Bay and Weeks Bay, this beach-house-turned-restaurant provides a Key West scene, with open decks, a screened porch, indoor and out-door bars, and a dining room. On the menu you'll find plenty of steamed fresh seafood. Try the steamed Royal Red shrimp, served with potato salad, corn, cole slaw, and garlic bread. There's open-air dining on the deck or porch, and live music on Friday, Saturday, and Sunday afternoons. *$13–$20. 10299 County Rd. 1, Fairhope 36532, tel. 251/928–1747. AE, D, DC, MC, V.*

✪ **WASH HOUSE** This hidden-away, intimate restaurant is housed behind the Punta Clara Kitchen in the rustic building that once served as that Victorian home's kitchen and washhouse. Tables with candlelight, and a large brick fireplace make it an especially romantic dinner spot. Be sure to consider the nightly specials—there are usually as many specials as regular items offered on the menu. Try the catch of the day, which is often the very popular pan-seared grouper. *$18–$30. 1711 U.S. 98, Point Clear 36564, tel. 251/928–4838. AE, D, DC, MC, V. No lunch.*

SLEEP

✪ **BAY BREEZE BED & BREAKFAST** A winding white-shell driveway leads through a camellia and azalea garden to this stucco-and-wood B&B owned by Bill and Becky Jones. The property, which was Becky's childhood home, fronts Mobile Bay not far from downtown Fairhope and has a 462-foot-long pier for fishing, crabbing, sunbathing, or just relaxing (sometimes breakfast is served at the end of the pier). Bedrooms in the main house have wood floors, brass queen-size beds, and antique furnishings. The cottage suites are light and spacious. *$130, $145 suites, $160 cottages. 742 S. Mobile St., Fairhope 36533, tel. 251/928–8976 or 866/ 928–8976, fax 251/929–2389, www.bbonline. 1 room; 2 suites; 2 cottages. Fans, some kitchenettes, cable TV, fishing, bicycles, recreation room, some pets allowed; no kids under 18, no smoking. AE, MC, V. BP.*

CHURCH STREET INN ♦ In the center of town, this early 1900s home is listed on the National Register of Historic Places. Restored throughout, this home contains five generations of family antiques and heirlooms. There's a large living room, a front porch lined with high-back rockers, and a garden courtyard. Each guest bedroom is furnished in period antiques, and each has its own private bath. Three blocks away you'll find Mobile Bay and several miles of public beaches, rose gardens, and parks. *$120. 51 S. Church St., Fairhope 36533, tel. 251/928–8976 or 866/928–8976, fax 251/929–2389. 3 rooms. Cable TV; no kids under 18. AE, MC, V. BP.*

HOLIDAY INN EXPRESS ♦ This standard inn is right on U.S. 98, close to Fairhope shops, restaurants, and a golf course. It's 20 minutes from downtown Mobile. *$75–$89. 19751 Greeno Rd., Fairhope 36532, tel. 251/928–9191, fax 251/990–7824, www.hiexpress.com. 65 rooms. Complimentary Continental breakfast, in-room data ports, refrigerators, cable TV, pool, laundry facilities, business services. AE, D, DC, MC, V.*

KEY WEST INN ♦ On U.S. 98 just 3 mi from downtown Fairhope, this inn's guest rooms have watercolor paintings by a local artist. *$52–$69; $85–$99 suites. 231 S. Greeno Rd., Fairhope 36532, tel. 251/990–7373 or 866/253–9937, fax 251/990–9671, www.keywestinn. net. 55 rooms; 8 suites. Complimentary Continental breakfast, in-room data ports, microwaves, refrigerators, cable TV, pool. AE, D, MC, V.*

✪ MARRIOTT'S GRAND HOTEL RESORT, GOLF CLUB & SPA Ensconced on 550 acres of beautifully landscaped grounds on Mobile Bay, the Grand has been a cherished landmark since 1847 and is one of the South's premier resorts. The octagonal, two-story, cypress-panel and -beam lobby serves as the hub for several wings. Its large three-sided fireplace, armchairs, and porcelain display evoke a casual elegance that is echoed in the half-moon dining room overlooking the bay. Amenities are added constantly; recent major improvements include a water park with fountains and geysers, a beach with a boat launch, and a European spa. The resort's Lakewood Golf Club is the southernmost link in the Robert Trent Jones Golf Trail. *$174–$194, $300 suites. 1 Grand Blvd., off Scenic 98, or 98 A, Point Clear 36564, tel. 251/928–9201 or 800/544–9933, fax 251/928–1149, www.marriottgrand.com. 405 rooms; 30 suites.*

5 restaurants, room service, in-room data ports, cable TV, 2 18-hole golf courses, 8 tennis courts, 2 pools, 2 hot tubs, sauna, spa, beach, boating, fishing, bicycles, horseback riding, lounge, baby-sitting, children's programs (ages 5–12), playground, laundry facilities, laundry service, business services, meeting rooms, no-smoking rooms. AE, D, DC, MC, V.

POINT OF VIEW GUESTHOUSE ♦ Built in the 1900s, this guest house faces the beach and has its own wharf and pier. The rooms are furnished with a combination of beach wicker and antique furniture. The property is on 3 acres of gardens, and is less than 3 mi from the town of Fairhope. *$120. 19493 Scenic Hwy. 98, Fairhope 36532, tel. 251/928–1809. 2 suites. Complimentary Continental breakfast, kitchenettes, cable TV, in-room VCRs, pool. AE, MC, V.*

MORE INFO

EASTERN SHORE CHAMBER OF COMMERCE ♦ *327 Fairhope Ave., Fairhope 36532, tel. 251/928–6387, fax 251/928–6389. www. eschamber.com.*

GETTING HERE

From I–10 take Exit 35 onto U.S. 98 S to reach Fairhope and Point Clear.

GULF SHORES & ORANGE BEACH

With white sand and gentle warm water, the Gulf Coast is by far one of the state's greatest attractions. The cooling offshore breezes provide a respite from the hot, humid temperatures found around Alabama in summer. Although the Gulf Shores beach area has plenty of concessions and is usually crowded, it's not impossible to find an isolated beach walk—you need only venture a few miles west. To the east of Gulf Shores is Orange Beach, a heavily developed coastal strip between the Gulf of Mexico and Perdido Bay, with its peaceful bayous and creeks. Both towns are separated from the mainland by the Intracoastal Waterway—with 32 mi of white-sand beaches and things to do, from amusement parks to golf and minigolf, to sailboat charters.

SEE & DO

ALABAMA GULF COAST ZOO ♦ This is the place to explore the natural habitats of more than 250 animals. Elevated decks offer close-up views of all animals, from alligators to giraffes and lions. *1204 Gulf Shores Pkwy., 36542, tel. 251/968–5731, fax 251/968–5731, www.alabamagulfcoastzoo.com. $8.80. Memorial Day–Labor Day, daily 9–4:30; Labor Day–Memorial Day, daily 9–4.*

BON SECOUR NATIONAL WILDLIFE REFUGE ♦ Within the 6,700 acres of this refuge you'll find native and migratory birds and a number of endangered species, including the loggerhead sea turtle. You can hike or swim at some of the five units of the refuge. *12295 AL 180 W, Gulf Shores 36542, tel. 251/540–7720, bonsecour.fws.gov.*

FORT MORGAN ♦ Built in the early 1800s to guard the entrance to Mobile Bay, the fort saw fiery action during the Battle of Mobile Bay in 1864. Confederate torpedoes (floating mines) sank the ironclad *Tecumseh,* prompting Union admiral David Farragut to give his famous command: "Damn the torpedoes; Full speed ahead!" The fort's original outer walls still stand; outside the fort, in a separate building, a museum chronicles the fort's history and displays artifacts from Indian days through World War II, with an emphasis on the Civil War. *51 Hwy. 180 W, Gulf Shores 36542, tel. 251/540-7125. $5. Fort May–Oct., daily 8–7; Nov.–Feb., daily 8–5; Mar. and Apr., daily 8–6. Museum daily 9–5.*

✪ GULF STATE PARK Along with 2½ mi of pure white beaches and glimmering dunes, the park, covering 6,150 acres, has two freshwater lakes with fishing; plus you can bike, hike, and jog on trails through pine forests here. Near the large beach pavilion, a concrete fishing pier juts 825 feet into the Gulf. There are also a Gulf-front resort lodge and convention center, 468 campsites, and 21 cottages, plus tennis courts and a golf course. *20115 AL 135, Gulf Shores 36542, tel. 251/948–7275, 800/544–4853, or 800/252–7275.*

☾ TRACK FAMILY RECREATION CENTER ♦ This popular amusement complex has go-karts, bumper boats, bungee jumping, and video arcades to keep your teens amused while the wee ones enjoy trains, swings, and a Ferris wheel. *3200 Gulf Shores Pkwy., 36542, tel. 251/968–8111, www.gulfcoastrooms.com/thetrack. Daily 10–10.*

☾ WATERVILLE USA ♦ There's a lot packed into these 17 acres: a wave pool with 3-foot waves, nine exciting water slides, and a lazy river ride around the park. For younger children there are gentler rides in a supervised play area. The adjacent amusement park has a 36-hole miniature golf course, a video-game arcade, and rides, such as a roller coaster, NASCAR go-karts, a kiddie area, laser tag, and a ride ejection seat—all priced per ride or game. Note that hours are seasonal, so dates change slightly from year to year. *906 Gulf Shores Pkwy. (AL 59), Gulf Shores 36542, tel. 251/948–2106, www.watervilleusa.com. $21 for water park, $13 for people under 42 inches tall; prices are per ride for amusement park; $30 for water park and unlimited rides in amusement park, $22 for people under 42 inches tall. Water park Memorial Day–mid-Aug., daily 10–6; mid-Aug.–Labor Day, weekends 10–6. Amusement park Mar.–Aug. 18, daily 10–midnight; Aug. 19–Sept., Thurs. and Sun. noon–8, Fri. and Sat. noon–10.*

SHOP

The more than 120 outlet stores in the **Riviera Centre,** 8 mi north of Gulf Shores, offer savings of up to 75% off regular retail prices. Stores include Danskin, Liz Claiborne, Bose, Coach, Bass Shoes, and Pfaltzgraff. *2601 AL 59 S, Foley 36535, tel. 251/943–8888, www.shoprivieracentre.com. Mon.–Sat. 10–9, Sun. 11–6.*

OUTDOORS

Freshwater and saltwater fishing in the Gulf area are excellent. Lovely **Gulf State Park** (20115 AL 135, 36542, tel. 251/948–7275), in Gulf Shores, has fishing from an 825-foot pier. Deep-sea fishing from charter boats is very popular but not a good idea if you tend to get seasick. You can also rent bicycles and follow one of the biking trails through the pine forests here.

In Gulf Shores, you can sign on board the *Wishbone* (tel. 251/981–3474) or one of many other charter boats for a full- or half-day fishing expedition. Catches from deep-sea expeditions include king mackerel, amberjack, tuna, white marlin, blue marlin, grouper, bonito, sailfish, and red snapper.

Coastal Alabama has developed into one of the nicest golfing destinations in the Southeast. More courses are opening, and the names of their architects read like a who's who of the golfing world—Robert Trent Jones Sr., Arnold Palmer, and Jerry Pate, for example. With winter temperatures averaging in the 60°F range and with pleasant breezes, the area has become a true year-round-fun spot. Prices for all the courses range from about $35 to $70 for greens fees and a cart.

The spectacular 18-hole, par-72 course at Kiva Dunes Golf & Beach Club, **Kiva Dunes** (13 mi west of Gulf Shores on AL 180, tel. 251/540–7000 or 888/733–5482, www.kivadunes.com), designed by Jerry Pate, combines oceanfront dunes golf with Scottish-style links golf. The **Craft Farms** complex (3840 Cotton Creek Blvd., off AL 59 north of Gulf Shores, tel. 251/968–7500 or 800/327–2657, www.craftfarms.com) has three 18-hole, par-72 courses: the Arnold Palmer–designed Cotton Creek and Cypress Bend; and the Larry Nelson–designed Woodlands course. About 12 mi north of Gulf Shores in Foley, the **Glenlakes Golf Club** (9530 Clubhouse Dr., tel. 251/955–1220, www.glenlakesgolf.com), a course designed by Bruce Devlin, has 18 challenging holes that play par-72 at just under 7,000 yards and another 9 holes that play par-35 stretching 3,100 yards. The 18-hole, par-72 course at **Gulf State Park** (20115 AL 135, tel. 251/948–7275), in Gulf Shores, is one of the area's oldest but most scenic and best-maintained courses along the coast.

The 53-foot catamaran *T. J. Spithre* (tel. 251/981–9706 for Island Sailing Center) can be rented with a captain. The *Daedalus* (tel. 251/987–1228) is a sailboat available for cruises in Gulf Shores. **Caribiana** (tel. 251/981–4442 or 888/203–4883) offers private, customized tours of the Perdido Bay area and its sand islands. Up to six people can be accommodated aboard a 23-foot sea skiff.

AFTER DARK

On the Alabama–Florida line is the sprawling **Flora-Bama Lounge** (17401 Perdido Key Dr., Pensacola, FL 32507, tel. 251/980–5118 or 850/492–3048, www.florabama.com), home of the annual Interstate Mullet Toss on the last full weekend in April. It's open 9 AM–2:30 AM, and the bar brings in live bands nightly. There's outdoor seating in summer.

EAT

✪ **BAYSIDE GRILL** For fine dining overlooking the back bays that channel to the Gulf, you can't beat this place. Seafood is the New Orleans–born chef's specialty, but you can also find pasta, steak, salads, and chicken, all served in large portions. The restaurant also serves a spectacular Sunday brunch. *$13–$22. 27842 Canal Rd., Orange Beach 36561, tel. 251/981–4899. AE, D, DC, MC, V.*

FLORA-BAMA LOUNGE ♦ Since 1962, this sprawling series of 10 bars and a package store and oyster bar has straddled the Alabama–Florida border, right on the Gulf of Mexico. Open 365 days a year and featuring live bands on three stages, the Flora-Bama epitomizes laid-back life at the beach. Try fresh oysters by the dozen and Royal Red shrimp by the pound; pizza and hot dogs are also on the menu. Rustic, casual setting with open-air dining on deck, live music nightly. *$4–$13. 17401 Perdido Key Dr., Pensacola, FL 32507, tel. 251/980–5118 or 850/492–3048, www.florabama.com. MC, V.*

GIFT HORSE ♦ Built as a hunting and fishing lodge in the early 1900s, this downtown Foley building has always been an important part of the community. In the 1940s, it was a USO (United Service Organizations) entertainment club for armed forces personnel; many 50th- and 60th-wedding anniversaries have been celebrated at the Gift Horse, where the couples met during World War II. The place is now known for its southern-style buffet with fried and baked chicken, tomato pie, and crawfish bisque. There's a kids' menu, and there's no smoking. *$12. 209 W. Laurel Ave., Foley 36535, tel. 251/943–3663. MC, V.*

HAZEL'S ♦ In a busy commercial resort area, this comfortable family restaurant is especially popular for its breakfast omelets. There's buffet dining for breakfast, lunch, and dinner. There's also an all-you-can-eat seafood buffet, featuring a variety of fish and shrimp, salads, gumbo, and oysters. They have a kids' menu, and Sunday brunch. *$15–$19. Rte. 182, Orange Beach 36561, tel. 251/ 981–4628. AE, D, DC, MC, V.*

KIRK KIRKLAND'S HITCHIN' POST ♦ This rustic, Western-theme restaurant has red-and-white-checked tablecloths, wooden floors, and a wide front porch with swings and rocking chairs. It attracts families and is known for daily lunch specials that include fried chicken, fried chicken strips, country fried steak, and sweet potatoes. Some seafood is also served: crab claws or shrimp, oysters, or fish fried or broiled. *$10–$20. 3401 Gulf Shores Pkwy. 36542, tel. 251/968–5041. AE, D, MC, V.*

LULU'S SUNSET GRILL ♦ With a famous brother lending celebrity status, and an enviable location on scenic Weeks Bay, Lucy Buffett—Jimmy's sister—can't miss with her laid-back restaurant. Fortunately, the food is as good as the setting and vibe. Start with the black-eyed-pea dip on crackers, and don't miss the blackened grouper po'boy topped with fried green tomato slices. *$7–$17. 11525 U.S. 98, Gulf Shores, tel. 251/990–9907. Reservations not accepted. AE, D, MC, V. Closed Mon.–Wed.*

MIKEE'S ♦ The food at this popular, no-nonsense seafood restaurant in the heart of Gulf Shores will be worth the inevitable wait. There's no view—it's a couple of blocks north of the beach—but while you wait, you can check out the photos of the owners' biggest catches among the other local memorabilia decorating the walls. The menu offers all-you-can-eat fried shrimp, steamed shrimp, barbecue shrimp, fried crab claws, and fried oysters, as well as po'boy sandwiches on New Orleans–style French bread. *$7–$20. 1st Ave. N and 2nd Ave. E, Gulf Shores 36542, tel. 251/948–6452. Reservations not accepted. AE, D, DC, MC, V.*

ORIGINAL OYSTER HOUSE ♦ Fishing photos and other memorabilia line the walls of this casual restaurant. Enjoy great bayou views while you dine on fresh local catch. Have your shrimp steamed, stuffed, blackened, grilled, or broiled—it's all available. Steak, chicken, and burgers are also on the menu. There is also a salad bar and a kids' menu. *$11–$18. 701 AL 59, at Bayou Village 36547, tel. 251/948–2445, www.theoysterhouse.com. AE, D, DC, MC, V.*

✪ THE OUTRIGGER This casual restaurant at the foot of Alabama Point Bridge has one of the best locations on the Alabama Gulf Coast. A wall of windows gives you a breathtaking view of the Gulf of Mexico. The menu includes fresh seafood, aged choice steaks, veal, and pasta. The restaurant is known for its creative sauces. There's a kids' menu, a patio for outdoor dining, and a full bar with an extensive wine list. *$13–$21. 27500 Perdido Beach Blvd., Orange Beach 32506, tel. 251/981–6700. AE, D, DC, MC, V.*

VOYAGERS ♦ Roses and art deco touches set the tone for this airy, elegant dining room. Two-level seating allows beach or poolside views from every table. Typical of chef Jim Freeman's dishes is pecan snapper. For dessert, the bread pudding soufflé in whisky sauce is quite fine. Service is deft, and there's an extensive wine selection. *$16–$30. Perdido Beach Resort, 27200 Perdido Beach Blvd., Orange Beach 36561, tel. 251/981–9811. Reservations essential. AE, D, DC, MC, V. Closed Mon. No lunch.*

ZEKE'S LANDING ♦ Large windows overlook Zeke's Landing Marina, where charter fishing boats arrive and depart. This two-story, casual restaurant specializes in seafood and also serves prime rib, rib eye, and pasta dishes. Dine outdoors on one of the three decks. The comfortable bar area is a great people-watching spot. There's a kids' menu and Sunday brunch. *$17–$25. 26649 Perdido Beach Blvd., Orange Beach 36561, tel. 251/981–4001, fax 251/981–2651. AE, D, DC, MC, V.*

SLEEP

BEACHSIDE RESORT HOTEL ♦ Directly on the Gulf of Mexico and within walking distance of Gulf Shores restaurants and nightlife, this hotel has a dramatic six-story atrium. All rooms have balconies and living rooms and most rooms face the Gulf. *$169–$179 rooms; $195 suites. 931 W. Beach Blvd., Gulf Shores 36547, tel. 251/948–6874 or 800/844–6913, fax 251/948–5232, www.qibeachside.com. 100 rooms; 51 suites. Restaurant, room service, some kitchenettes, cable TV, 2 pools, beach, 2 bars, playground, laundry facilities, business services, no-smoking rooms; no pets. AE, D, DC, MC, V.*

BEST WESTERN ON THE BEACH ♦ This motel overlooks the Gulf of Mexico and has a beachside pool with a rock waterfall and a children's wading pool. All rooms have private balconies. The honeymoon suite has a hot tub. The cost of beachfront rooms is significantly lower in winter. *$189–$300, suites $199–$310. 337 E. Beach Blvd., Gulf Shores 36542, tel. 251/948–2711 or 800/788–4557, fax 251/948–7339, www.bestwestern-onthebeach.com. 104 rooms; 2 suites. Restaurant, some kitchenettes, cable TV, 2 pools, 2 hot tubs, gym, beach, laundry facilities, business services. AE, D, DC, MC, V.*

GULF SHORES PLANTATION ♦ This large family resort, 13 mi west of Gulf Shores, faces the Gulf and has several condominium complexes as well as two-story duplex cottages of varying sizes—one can accommodate up to 33 people. Recreational activities abound, yet the remote location allows for peace and quiet. Next door, Kiva Dunes Golf Course is consistently ranked among the state's best by magazines such as *Golf Digest* and *Golf.* Note when asking for a room that standard doubles are called "suites," and larger rooms (really suites) are called "condos." *$132–154, suites $159–$195. AL 180 W, Box 1299, Gulf Shores 36542, tel. 251/540–5000 or 800/554–0344, fax 251/540–6055, www.gulfshoresplantation. com. 608 condos; 15 cottages. Café, kitchens, microwaves, refrigerators, cable TV, some in-room VCRs, 8 tennis courts, 6 pools (1 indoor), exercise equipment, hot tubs, saunas, steam rooms, beach, horseshoes, shuffleboard, volleyball, lounge, recreation room, shop, laundry facilities, no-smoking rooms. AE, D, MC, V.*

✪ **GULF STATE PARK RESORT HOTEL**   This modern, state-owned beachfront hotel is part of Gulf State Park, which occupies 6,150 acres, including a 2½-mi stretch of white-sand beach. All rooms face the beach, overlooking the Gulf of Mexico. An 825-foot state-operated fishing pier, the longest on the Gulf, is within easy walking distance. *$49–$113; $99–$214 suites. 21250 E. Beach Blvd., Gulf Shores 36535, tel. 251/948–4853 or 800/544–4853, fax 251/948–5998, www.dcnr.state.al.us/parks/gulf_1a.html. 144 rooms; 18 suites. Dining room, in-room data ports, some kitchenettes, cable TV, pool, driving range, 18-hole golf course, tennis court, beach, fishing, bar, laundry facilities, business services, no-smoking rooms. AE, MC, V.*

HILTON GARDEN INN ORANGE BEACH BEACHFRONT ♦ On the beach with beautiful Gulf views, this lushly landscaped hotel is near several golf courses, and only about 3 mi away from the nearest one. Nearby, on the beach, you can organize charter fishing and Jet Ski rentals. Each room has a private balcony, and some overlook the beach. The café is open for breakfast only. *$169–$359.*

23092 Perdido Beach Blvd., Orange Beach 36561, tel. 251/974–1600 or 888/644–5866, fax 251/974–1012, www.hiltongardeninn.com. 137 rooms. Café, in-room data ports, microwaves, refrigerators, cable TV, indoor-outdoor pool, hot tub, gym, beach, laundry facilities, business services, no-smoking rooms. AE, D, DC, MC, V.

HOLIDAY INN EXPRESS ♦ This standard inn is across from the Riviera Centre mall, 10 minutes from Gulf Shores. *$55–$119. 2682 S. McKenzie St., Foley 36535, tel. 251/943–9100 or 800/962–1833, fax 251/943–9421, www.hiexpress.com. 83 rooms. Complimentary Continental breakfast, microwaves, refrigerators, pool, gym, hot tub, laundry facilities, business services, no-smoking rooms. AE, D, DC, MC, V.*

✪ **ISLAND HOUSE HOTEL** Each room in this sleek, geometrically shaped hotel has a private balcony with a beautiful view of the pool area, white-sand beach, and the Gulf of Mexico. The hotel has 336 feet of private beach and is across from Zeke's Landing and Marina. Several malls and restaurants are within walking distance, 1 mi from Perdido Key. *$149, 2-night minimum stay in summer. 26650 Perdido Beach Blvd., Orange Beach 36535, tel. 251/981–6100 or 800/264–2642, fax 251/981–6543, www.islandhousehotel.com. 161 rooms. Room service, in-room data ports, in-room safes, cable TV, pool, wading pool, beach, bar, laundry facilities, business services, no-smoking rooms. AE, MC, V.*

ORIGINAL ROMAR HOUSE ♦ This simple beach cottage is filled with surprises—from the Caribbean-style upstairs sitting area to the Purple Parrot Bar to the art deco guest rooms, each with a private bath. *$79–$140. 23500 Perdido Beach Blvd., Orange Beach 36561, tel. 251/974–1625 or 800/487–6627, fax 251/974–1163, www.bbonline.com/al/romarhouse. 7 rooms. Hot tub, beach, bicycles, bar; no kids under 12, no smoking. AE, MC, V. BP.*

PERDIDO BEACH RESORT ♦ The 9- and 10-story towers of this resort are Mediterranean stucco and red tile. The lobby has marble floors and is decorated with a brass sculpture of gulls in flight and mosaics by Venetian artists. Rooms are furnished in comfortable coastal style, and all have a beach views and balconies. *$190–200, suites $405–$415. 27200 Perdido Beach Blvd., Orange Beach 36561, tel. 251/981–9811 or 800/634–8001, fax 251/981–5670, www.perdidobeachresort.com. 334 rooms; 13 suites. Restaurant, cable TV with movies, 4 tennis courts, indoor-outdoor pool, health club, 2 hot tubs, beach, bar, lobby lounge, lounge, laundry service, meeting rooms, no-smoking rooms. AE, D, DC, MC, V.*

SLEEP INN GULF FRONT RESORT ♦ Some rooms in this six-story hotel overlook the beach; all have balconies. *$45–$150. 25400 Perdido Beach Blvd., 36561, tel. 251/981–6722 or 800/430–2738, fax 251/981–6731, www.sleepinn.com. 118 rooms. Complimentary Continental breakfast, in-room data ports, some microwaves, some refrigerators, cable TV, pool, beach; no pets. AE, D, DC, MC, V.*

SUPER 8 ♦ Eight miles from the beach at Gulf Shores, this standard inn is also within a mile of Riviera Centre outlet mall, a 12-cinema movie theater, and numerous restaurants. There are no-smoking buildings. *$79–$89. 1517 S. McKenzie St., Foley 36535, tel. 251/943–3297, fax 251/943–7548, www.super8.com. 90 rooms in 3 buildings. Complimentary Continental breakfast, cable TV, pool, gym, business services, no-smoking rooms. AE, D, MC, V.*

WINFIELD RESORT HOTEL ♦ A three-story white stucco building facing the beach, this inn has an open atrium with a large balcony, overlooking the pool. The beach front rooms also have balconies and open onto the beach. *$69–$169. 22988 Perdido Beach Blvd., 36561, tel. 251/974–1598 or 888/485–3726, fax 251/974–1599, www.winfieldresorts.com. 97 rooms. Picnic area, complimentary Continental breakfast, in-room data ports, microwaves, refrigerators, cable TV, pool, beach, laundry facilities, business services, free parking; no pets. AE, D, DC, MC, V.*

MORE INFO

ALABAMA GULF COAST CONVENTION & VISITORS BUREAU ♦
3150 Gulf Shores Pkwy., Gulf Shores 36542, tel. 251/968–7511 or 800/745–7263, www.gulfshores.com.

GETTING HERE

To reach Gulf Shores and Orange Beach from I–10, take Exit 44 onto AL 59 South. AL 180 and AL 182 are the main beach routes between Gulf Shores and Orange Beach.

MOBILE

Fort Condé was the name given by the French in 1711 to the site known today as Mobile; around it blossomed the first white settlement in what is now Alabama. For eight years it was the capital of the French colonial empire, and it remained under French control until 1763, long after the capital had moved to New Orleans.

Mobile, a busy international port, is noted for its tree-lined boulevards fanning westward from the riverfront. In the heart of busy downtown is Bienville Square, a park with an ornate cast-iron fountain and shaded by centuries-old live oaks. One of the city's main thoroughfares, Dauphin Street, has many thriving restaurants, bars, and shops.

SEE & DO

✪ **BELLINGRATH GARDENS AND HOME** One of the most popular gardens in the South is Bellingrath, famous for its magnificent azaleas, which are part of 65 acres of gardens set amid a 905-acre semitropical landscape. Show time for the azaleas is mid- to late-March, when some 250,000 plantings of 200 different species are ablaze with color. But Bellingrath is a year-round wonder, with more than 75 varieties of roses blooming in summer, 60,000 chrysanthemum plants cascading in the fall, and red fields of poinsettias brightening the winter. At the annual Magic Christmas in Lights event, holiday decorations in the gardens light up the night throughout December. Countless species and flowering plants spring up along the Fowl River, surrounding streams, and a lake populated by ducks and swans. A free map lets you plan your own strolls along flagstone paths and across charming bridges. In April and October, large numbers of migratory birds drop by.

Coca-Cola bottling pioneer Walter D. Bellingrath began the nucleus of the gardens in 1917, when he and his wife bought a large tract of land to use as a fishing camp. But their travels prompted them to create, instead, a garden rivaling some they had seen in Europe, and in 1932 they opened it to the public. Today the brick home they built is open to visitors and has a fine collection of antiques, including the world's largest display of Boehm porcelain birds. Forty-five minute **boat cruises** on the Fowl River aboard the *Southern Belle* leave from the dock next to the Bellingrath Home daily at 10, noon, and 2 from mid-February through Thanksgiving. To reach Theodore from Mobile, take I–10 West to Exit 15, then follow CR 59 South to Theodore. *12401 Bellingrath Gardens Rd., Theodore, tel. 251/973–2217 or 800/247–8420,* Southern Belle *251/973–1244, fax 251/973–0540, www.bellingrath.org. Gardens $9.00; gardens and home $16.50; value pack, $25 for gardens, home, and cruise. Gardens daily 8–5; home open daily 9–4.*

✪ **BRAGG-MITCHELL MANSION** The mansion is one of the Gulf Coast's grandest structures and Mobile's most-photographed building. Built in 1855, the 20-room mansion is framed by 16 slender fluted columns. Mirrors in the double parlors are among the few original furnishings. *1906 Springhill Ave., 36607, tel. 251/471–6364, fax 251/478–3800, www.braggmitchellmansion.com. $5. Tues.–Fri. 10–3:30.*

CATHEDRAL-BASILICA OF THE IMMACULATE CONCEPTION ♦ Built on Spanish burial grounds, the Roman Basilica–designed cathedral stands in the heart of Mobile's Old Town. Construction began in 1835 and was completed in 1850. The cathedral features 14 hand-painted stations of the cross and underwent a major renovation in 2003. *2 S. Claiborne St., 36602, tel. 251/434–1565, fax 251/434–1588. Free. Weekdays 8:15–noon and 12:45–3.*

CONDÉ-CHARLOTTE MUSEUM HOUSE ♦ This house, next to Fort Condé, was built in 1822–24 as Mobile's first official jail. Its rooms now reflect the city's long history; each is furnished in a different period style, including French Empire, 18th-century British, and American Federal. *104 Theatre St., 36602, tel. 251/432–4722. $5. Tues.–Sat. 10–4.*

FORT CONDÉ ♦ In the center of town, this fort survives as a reminder of the city's beginnings, thanks to a reconstruction (one-third of the original size) that preserved it when its remains were discovered—150 years after the fort was destroyed—during the building of the I–10 interchange. A portion of the fort, originally built in 1724–35, houses the **visitor center** for the city, as well as a museum. Among the many brochures at the center are ones outlining excellent walking tours of the city's historic districts, including De Tonti Square, Church Street East, and Dauphin Street. *150 S. Royal St., 36602, tel. 251/208–7304. Free. Daily 8–5.*

☾ GULF COAST EXPLOREUM SCIENCE CENTER AND IMAX DOME THEATER ♦ This science museum, across from the Mobile Convention Center downtown, has a very popular Hands On Hall, where kids of all ages can have fun while learning through interactive exhibits, and a new Minds On Hall, which focuses on the brain. Films in the state-of-the-art IMAX Dome Theater change every few months. Parking is at a premium in this area, you can park in the lot across from Fort Condé off Royal Street. *65 Government St., 36602, tel. 251/208–6883 or 877/625–4386, www.exploreum.net. Exhibits $7.75; IMAX theater $7.75; both $12. Winter–spring, weekdays 9–5, Sat. 10–5, Sun. noon–5; fall, Tues.–Fri. 9–5, Sat. 10–5, Sun. noon–5.*

MOBILE MUSEUM OF ART ♦ A major expansion in recent years tripled show space at this increasingly ambitious facility and brought several major exhibits to Mobile, including a retrospective of Depression-era art and a traveling collection from the Vatican. The impressive permanent collection houses some 6,000 pieces of mostly American art. *Langdan Park, 4850 Museum Dr., 36608, tel. 251/208–5200, www.mobilemuseumofart.com. $6. Mon.–Sat. 10–6, Sun. noon–5.*

MUSEUM OF MOBILE ♦ In the former Southern Market–Old City Hall building next to the Gulf Coast Exploreum, the museum has interactive exhibits that tell Mobile's history from the founding of the French settlement of Fort Louis de la Mobile to Mobile Bay's involvement in the Civil War to the most notorious hurricanes in the past century. *111 S. Royal St., tel. 251/208–7569, www. museumofmobile.com. $10. Mon.–Sat. 9–5, Sun. 1–5.*

NATIONAL AFRICAN-AMERICAN ARCHIVES AND MUSEUM ♦ This modest museum holds portraits and biographies of well-known African-Americans. There's also a collection of carvings and artifacts, including Mardi Gras costumes, documents, and books. *564 Dr. Martin Luther King Jr. Ave., 36603, tel. 251/433–8511. Donations accepted. Weekdays 8–4, Sat. 10–2, Sun. by appointment only.*

OAKLEIGH HOUSE MUSEUM ♦ The **Oakleigh Garden Historic District** begins 1 mi southwest of Fort Condé; signs lead to Oakleigh, an antebellum Greek Revival mansion with a stairway circling under ancient live oaks to a small portico. The high-ceiling, half-timber house was built between 1833 and 1838 and is typical of the most expensive dwellings of its day. Fine period furniture, portraits, silver, jewelry, kitchen implements, toys, and more are displayed. Next door is the **Cox-Deasy House,** a raised creole cottage built in 1850 that is a more typical middle-class home. Also on the property is the **Mardi Gras Cottage,** filled with quilts and other artifacts from the 19th and 20th centuries. Members of the Historic Mobile Preservation Society conduct tours. *350 Oakleigh Pl., 36604, tel. 251/432–1281, www.historicmobile.org. $7 for all three homes. Tues.–Sat. 9–3:30.*

PHOENIX FIRE MUSEUM ♦ Dating from 1855 and once home to the Phoenix Fire Company, the restored firehouse holds steamers and fire engines, dating back to the 19th century. Exhibits showcase the men and equipment that fought the city's early fires. *203 S. Claiborne St., 36602, tel. 251/208–7554, fax 251/208–7686, www.museumofmobile.com. Free. Tues.–Sat. 9–5, Sun. 1–5.*

RICHARDS–DAR HOUSE MUSEUM ♦ In the **DeTonti Square Historic District,** this Italianate house, built in 1860, holds magnificent period furnishings. Note the white lace ironwork outside the brick town house. The Daughters of the American Revolution administer this welcoming museum, which serves tea and cookies. *256 N. Joachim St., tel. 251/208–7320, www.gulftel.com/asdar/richards.htm. $5. Weekdays 11–3:30, Sat. 10–4, Sun. 1–4.*

STATE STREET A.M.E. ZION CHURCH ♦ This is one of the oldest and most striking African Methodist Episcopal Zion churches in town. *502 State St., tel. 251/432–3965.*

ST. LOUIS STREET MISSIONARY BAPTIST CHURCH ♦ The conference that established Selma University was held here. *108 N. Dearborn St., tel. 251/438–3823.*

UNIVERSITY OF SOUTH ALABAMA ♦ With some 12,000 students at its west Mobile campus, the university is a major center for undergraduate, graduate, and professional study. Also here are a College of Medicine and clinical facilities. The Jaguars boast a top collegiate baseball program with NCAA tournament appearances in each of the last nine seasons. *307 University Blvd., 36688, tel. 251/460–6101, fax 251/460–7827, www.southalabama.edu. Free. Daily.*

✪ **USS *ALABAMA*** The ship is anchored in Mobile Bay just east of downtown Mobile off I–10. Public subscription saved the mighty gray battleship from being scrapped ignominiously after her heroic World War II service, which ranged from Scapa Flow to the South Pacific. A tour of the ship gives a fascinating look into the life of a 2,500-member crew. Anchored next to the battleship is the submarine **USS *Drum*,** another active battle weapon during World War II, also open to visitors. Other exhibits in the 100-acre **Battleship Memorial Park** include an A-12 Blackbird spy plane and a P-51 Mustang fighter plane. *2703 Battleship Pkwy. (U.S. 90), 36601, tel. 251/433–2703 or 800/426–4929, www.ussalabama.com. $10, parking $2. Apr.–Sept., daily 8–6, Oct.–Mar., daily 8–4.*

WILDLAND EXPEDITIONS ◆ Led by Captain Gene Burrell aboard his self-designed boat, tours take you into the Mobile-Tensaw Delta Swamp, with close-up views of plants and animals. During warm months, it's possible to spot alligators. Captain Burrell's expertise enlivens explorations. *Chickasaw Marina, U.S. 43, tel. 251/460–8206. $20. Feb.–Dec., Tues.–Sat. 10 and 2.*

SHOP

Most shopping in Mobile is in malls and shopping centers in the suburban areas. Stores are generally open Monday–Saturday 10–9, Sunday 1–6. Sales tax is 9%.

Antiques buffs love Mobile because it offers more than 25 individual shops and malls that specialize in antiques. In the Loop area of midtown (where Government Street, Airport Boulevard, and Dauphin Island Parkway converge), several shops are within walking distance. The seemingly endless **Antiques at the Loop** (2103 Airport Blvd., 36606, tel. 251/476–0309) has lamps, stained glass, furnishings, and garden accessories. The **Cotton City Antique Mall** (2012 Airport Blvd., 36606, tel. 251/479–9747) offers

12,000 square feet of antique furniture, vintage linens, clocks, and more. The **Red Barn Antique Mall** (418 Dauphin Island Pkwy., 36606, tel. 251/473–9227) has at least 15 shops with antiques, from glassware and books to furniture. **Yellow House Antiques** (1902 Government St., 36606, tel. 251/476–7382) is an upscale shop with 18th- and 19th-century English, Continental, and American furniture and accessories.

Colonial Mall Bel Air (Airport Blvd. and I–65, tel. 251/478–1893) has 130 stores, including JCPenney, Parisian, Target, Dillard's, and Sears Roebuck. Directly across the street from the Colonial Mall Bel Air, **Springdale Mall** (Airport Blvd. and I–65, tel. 251/471–1945, www.springdalemall.com), anchored by McRae's, has dozens of stores, including Best Buy, Linens and Things, and Barnes and Noble.

OUTDOORS

The 18-hole, par-72 **Azalea City Golf Course** (1000 Gaillard Dr., 36608, tel. 251/342–4221) is operated by the city of Mobile. **Magnolia Grove** (7001 Magnolia Grove Pkwy., 36618, tel. 251/645–0075 or 800/949–4444), part of the Robert Trent Jones Golf Trail, has 54 holes of championship golf: two par-72 courses and an 18-hole, par-54 (each hole is par 3) course that is anything but easy. **Rock Creek** (140 Clubhouse Dr., 36533, tel. 251/928–4223, www.rockcreekgolf.com), in Fairhope, on the eastern shore of Mobile Bay, has 18 holes and is par 72. **TimberCreek** (9650 TimberCreek Blvd., tel. 251/621–9900), in Daphne, has 27 holes and is par 72.

The **Mobile BayBears** (755 Bolling Brothers Blvd., off I–65 at the Government Blvd. exit, 36606, tel. 251/479–2327, www.mobilebaybears.com), the AA affiliate of the San Diego Padres, play baseball from April through October at "the Hank"—Hank Aaron Stadium, named for the baseball legend and Mobile native.

At the **Mobile Greyhound Park** (Theodore-Dawes Rd. at Exit 13 off I–10 W, tel. 251/653–5000, www.mobilegreyhoundpark.com), about 10 mi from Mobile, there are pari-mutuel betting (a cooperative betting procedure) and a restaurant overlooking the finish line. The track offers simulcasts. The minimum age for admission is 18.

AFTER DARK

The **Joe Jefferson Players** (tel. 251/471–1534), an amateur group started more than 50 years ago, performs plays and musicals at the **Joe Jefferson Playhouse** (11 S. Carlen St., tel. 251/471–1534, www.jjp.net). The **Mitchell Center** (Old Shell Rd., at the University of South Alabama, tel. 251/460–6101, www.mitchellcenter.com), home to the university's Jaguars basketball team, hosts concerts and other special events throughout the year. In the lobby the spectacular restored 1940s Waterman Globe, 12 feet in diameter, rotates at the same angle as the Earth's axis. The **Mobile Civic Center** (401 Civic Center Dr., tel. 251/208–7261, www.mobilecivicctr.com) presents theater groups, orchestras, and concerts of all kinds. Near the Mobile Museum of Art, the Playhouse in the Park's **Pixie Players** (Langdan Park, tel. 251/344–1537) is a children's theater company that puts on five shows annually. The 1927 **Saenger Theater** (6 S. Joachim St., tel. 251/208–5600, www.mobilesaenger.com) hosts orchestras and touring companies.

Much of Mobile's nightlife centers around downtown's former commercial district, **Dauphin Street,** which today has a number of restaurants and nightspots spread out over several blocks. Mobilians have taken to calling the area LoDa, short for Lower Dauphin. In midtown Mobile, the **Double Olive** (2033 Airport Blvd., tel. 251/450–5001, www.doubleolive.com) is an artsy, urbane martini bar that draws hip crowds. Former LoDa landmark

Drayton Place (828 S. Beltline Hwy., 36609, tel. 251/342–1870, www.draytonplace.com) has moved a few miles to the southwest, but it still offers a vast selection of imported beers at its over-size bar, as well as Creole-inspired cuisine for lunch, dinner, or Sunday jazz brunch. In the back, there's a billiards table; bands play live music on Thursday through Saturday nights. **Monsoon's** (210 Dauphin St., tel. 251/433–3500) is one of several al-most indistinguishable bars that host local bands as well as a few national ones, drawing crowds of twentysomethings on Friday and Saturday nights.

EAT

BRICK PIT ♦ It's "the best damn barbecue in the state of Al-abama," owner Bill Armbrecht insists. Chicken, ribs, and pork are smoked for hours over a blend of hickory and pecan to achieve a distinct flavor. Barbecue sauce comes spicy or sweet, with soft white bread for dipping. Be sure to add your name to the graffiti scrawled in red marker all over the walls and ceiling. Try the smoked pulled-pork plate. *$7–$12. 5456 Old Shell Rd., 36608, tel. 251/343–0001, www.brickpit.com. MC, V. Closed Sun. and Mon.*

DEW DROP INN ♦ Mobile's oldest restaurant, a no-frills eatery, is also one of the city's most popular places to meet. The best-loved item on the menu is the Dew Drop Inn hot dog, which goes well with homemade onion rings or thick-cut steak fries. Daily specials include down-home favorites, such as fried chicken or catfish, ac-companied by perfectly seasoned vegetables. *$2–$15. 1808 Old Shell Rd., 36607, tel. 251/473–7872. Reservations not accepted. AE, MC, V. Closed Sun. No dinner Sat.*

FELIX'S FISH CAMP ♦ It's just five minutes from downtown on the causeway, and its large windows overlook Mobile Bay with a view of the Battleship USS *Alabama* and the downtown Mobile skyline.

Menu items include seafood, shrimp and crab fettuccine, along with chicken and steak entrées. *$10–$20. 1420 Battleship Pkwy., 36601, tel. 251/626–6710. AE, D, MC, V.*

✪ **JUSTINE'S AT THE PILLARS** When chef Matt Shipp acquired the Pillars, one of Mobile's most beloved fine-dining landmarks, the city breathed a collective sigh of relief, knowing the restaurant would be in good hands. Shipp, a Mobile native who trained in kitchens from New York to New Orleans, earned his local reputation at his Justine's Courtyard and Carriageway downtown before closing that establishment and moving to this pinnacle of Mobile's dining scene. With Justine's at the Pillars, housed in a midtown mansion, he's continuing the tradition of excellent service and the finest in steaks and seafood, but has added his own Gulf Coast favorites, such as turtle soup. *$12–$25. 1757 Government St., 36604, tel. 251/471–3411, www.justinesrestaurant.com. AE, D, DC, MC, V. Closed Sun. No lunch Sat.*

✪ **LORETTA'S** At a colorful corner a block off Dauphin Street, this place has its own dramatic flair. It's hidden behind a wall of glass covered in creeping fig, with a unique style—gleaming silver palm trees and whimsical, mismatched salt and pepper shakers. In the kitchen, owner-chef Christopher Hunter adds creative nuances to Southern favorites, such as sausage-stuffed pork loin and pan-seared sashimi tuna steak. *$10–$22. 19 S. Conception St., 36602, tel. 251/432–2200. AE, D, DC, MC, V. No lunch weekends, no dinner Sun.–Tues.*

THE MARINER ♦ Enjoy a view of boats traveling under the Dog River Bridge and across Mobile Bay at this rambling waterfront restaurant. On the menu are shrimp, oysters, snow crab, grouper, and meats, such as rib-eye steak. Try the fried crab claws. There's open-air dining on deck, and a kids' menu. *$10–$15. 6036 Rock Point Rd., 36605, tel. 251/443–5700. AE, D, MC, V. No lunch Mon.–Sat.*

ROUSSOS RESTAURANT ♦ With a nautical look created by lots of fishnets and scenes of ships at sea, this place serves seafood fried, broiled, or served Greek style (with a blend of spices and oils). Steaks and chicken also are available. The appetizers are big favorites—especially the baked oysters and seafood gumbo. *$10–$20. 166 S. Royal St., 36602, tel. 251/433–3322. AE, D, DC, MC, V. Closed Sun.*

RUTH'S CHRIS STEAK HOUSE ♦ Although it specializes in steaks—corn-fed, aged beef broiled to juicy perfection—this fine-dining establishment, in midtown Mobile, also offers a variety of fresh seafood dishes, veal chops, and broiled chicken. *$30–$40. 271 Glenwood St., 36606, tel. 251/476–0516. www.ruthschris.com. AE, D, DC, MC, V. No lunch.*

SLEEP

✪ **ADAM'S MARK MOBILE** This 28-story riverfront hotel, completely renovated in 2002, is connected to the Mobile Convention Center by a covered skywalk. The large guest rooms have floor-to-ceiling windows with views of downtown Mobile or Mobile Bay, and standard chain hotel–style furniture. The Riverview Cafe and Grill specializes in Gulf Coast seafood; lighter fare and live entertainment are offered six nights a week in the Tiffany Rose Restaurant. Rates here vary according to how full the hotel is, so if you're here during a convention, expect to pay more for the same room. *$95–$170, suites $215–$450. 64 S. Water St., 36602, tel. 251/438–4000 or 866/749–6069, fax 251/415–3060, www.adamsmark.com. 377 rooms; 12 suites. 2 restaurants, room service, in-room data ports, minibars, cable TV, pool, health club, hot tub, sauna, bar, dry cleaning, business services, meeting rooms, no-smoking rooms. AE, D, DC, MC, V.*

AIRPORT PLAZA MOBILE ♦ Close to malls and restaurants, this hotel caters to business travelers, but also attracts leisure travelers thanks to its putting course and pool. To get here from I–65, take Exit 3 (Airport Boulevard) from either direction, then head west and take a right at the sign for West Service Road—the hotel is on the right. *$59–$79. 600 S. Beltline Hwy., 36608, tel. 251/344–8030 or 800/752–0398, fax 251/344–8055, www.airportplazamobile.com. 236 rooms. Restaurant, room service, in-room data ports, cable TV, 3-hole putting green, 2 tennis courts, 2 pools (1 indoor), wading pool, gym, hot tub, bar, business services, convention center, meeting rooms, airport shuttle. AE, D, DC, MC, V.*

DRURY INN ♦ This inn is right off I–65 and Airport Boulevard (Exit 3 from the interstate). It's next to a 24-hour restaurant, and close to Bel Air and Springdale malls. *$72. 824 S. Beltline Hwy., 36609, tel. 251/344–7700 or 800/325–8300, fax 251/344–7700, www.druryhotels.com. 110 rooms. Complimentary Continental breakfast, in-room data ports, cable TV, pool, gym, laundry facilities, business services, some pets allowed, no-smoking rooms. AE, D, DC, MC, V.*

HAMPTON INN ♦ With easy access to I–65, this standard inn is centrally located near Airport Boulevard and the Mobile business district. *$63. 930 S. Beltline Hwy., 36609, tel. 251/344–4942, fax 251/341–4520, www.hamptoninn.com. 118 rooms. Complimentary Continental breakfast, in-room data ports, cable TV, pool, business services, no-smoking rooms. AE, D, DC, MC, V.*

HOLIDAY INN ♦ This inn with standard rooms done in burgundy floral patterns is fully equipped with plenty of facilities to keep you comfortable. They also have package rates if you plan on going to Bellingrath Gardens. *$69–$109. 5465 U.S. 90 W, Mobile 36619, tel. 866/436–4329 or 251/666–5600, fax 251/666–2773, www.holiday-inn.com. 159 rooms. Restaurant, room service, in-room data ports, microwaves, refrigerators, cable TV, pool, gym, hot tub, bar,* *laundry facilities, business services, airport shuttle, some pets allowed, no-smoking rooms. AE, D, DC, MC, V.*

LA QUINTA ♦ This standard inn is along I–65 at busy Airport Boulevard, a mile from Bel Air and Springdale malls and close to many restaurants. *$62–$69. 816 S. Beltline Hwy., 36609, tel. 251/ 343–4051 or 800/531–5900, fax 251/343–2897, www.laquinta.com. 122 rooms. Complimentary Continental breakfast, in-room data ports, cable TV, pool, laundry service, business services, some pets allowed, no-smoking rooms. AE, D, DC, MC, V.*

LAFAYETTE PLAZA ♦ This hotel in the heart of downtown Mobile's business and historic districts is within walking distance of the Museum of Mobile, Phoenix Fire Museum, Gulf Coast Exploreum, and more. The rooftop lounge offers breathtaking views of the city and the waterfront. *$59–$89. 301 Government St., 36602, tel. 251/694–0100 or 800/692–6662, fax 251/694–0160, www. lafayetteplazahotel.com. 210 rooms. Restaurant, bar, in-room data ports, cable TV, pool, hair salon, bar, lounge, laundry service, business services, some pets allowed (fee), no-smoking rooms. AE, D, DC, MC, V.*

✪ **MALAGA INN** A delightful, romantic getaway, this place comprises two town houses built by a wealthy landowner in 1862. The lobby is furnished with 19th-century antiques and opens onto a landscaped central courtyard with a fountain. The rooms are large, airy, and furnished with antiques. The Malaga is on a quiet street downtown, within walking distance of the Museum of Mobile and the Gulf Coast Exploreum. *$79, suites $150. 359 Church St., 36602, tel. 800/235–1586 or 251/438–4701, tel./fax 251/438– 4701, www.malagainn.com. 35 rooms; 3 suites. Cable TV, pool, lounge, business services. AE, D, MC, V.*

MOBILE AIRPORT DAYS INN ♦ This standard inn is right at I–65 and Airport Boulevard. It's close to Springdale Mall, Bel Air Mall, and convenient to other shops and many restaurants. *$49. 3650*

Airport Blvd., 36608, tel. 251/344–3410, fax 251/344–8790, www. daysinn.com. 162 rooms. In-room data ports, cable TV, pool, business services, no-smoking rooms. AE, D, DC, MC, V.

MOBILE MARRIOTT ♦ This 20-story hotel is in midtown Mobile east of I–65, near Bel Air Mall and several restaurants. *$59–$99. 3101 Airport Blvd., 36606, tel. 251/476–6400, fax 251/476–9360, www.marriott.com. 250 rooms. Restaurant, in-room data ports, cable TV, pool, hot tub, bar, laundry service, business services, airport shuttle, no-smoking floors, no-smoking rooms. AE, D, DC, MC, V.*

RADISSON ADMIRAL SEMMES HOTEL ♦ This restored 1940 hotel in the historic district is a favorite with local politicians. It's also popular with party goers, particularly during Mardi Gras, because of its excellent location directly on the parade route. The spacious, high-ceiling rooms have a burgundy-and-green color scheme and are furnished in Queen Anne and Chippendale styles. Ask about the Supersaver Family rates, which are about $79 for two double beds ($99 with breakfast). *$142, suites $195. 251 Government St., 36602, tel. 251/432–8000 or 800/333–3333, fax 251/ 405–5942, www.radisson.com/mobileal. 148 rooms; 22 suites. Restaurant, pool, bar, business services. AE, D, DC, MC, V.*

RAMADA INN AND SUITES ♦ A solid choice in a good location, this corporate outpost is along I–10 in the Tillman's Corner area, 2 mi from Mobile Greyhound Park, 10 mi from downtown Mobile, and 15 mi from Mobile Municipal Airport. There are no-smoking rooms among its simply, comfortably furnished units. *$54 rooms; $64 suites. 5472-A Inn Rd., 36614, tel. 251/660–1520, fax 251/ 666–4240, www.ramada.com. 105 rooms; 15 suites. Some microwaves, some refrigerators, cable TV, pool, business services, meeting room, some pets allowed (fee), no-smoking rooms. AE, D, DC, MC, V.*

RED ROOF INN MOBILE–SOUTH ♦ In the Tillman's Corner area off I–10, this standard inn is about 18 mi from Bellingrath Gardens and Home, 10 mi from downtown Mobile, and 30 mi from

Dauphin Island. *$41. 5450 Coca-Cola Rd., 36619, tel. 251/666–1044, fax 251/666–1032, www.redroof.com. 108 rooms. In-room data ports, cable TV, business services, some pets allowed, no-smoking rooms. AE, D, DC, MC, V.*

✪ **TOWLE HOUSE** Built in 1874, this lovely bed-and-breakfast is in the Old Dauphinway Historic District, one block from oak tree–lined Government Street and close to downtown Mobile. Rooms are furnished with antiques and have private baths. Breakfast is served in the elegant dining room on china with sterling silver; afternoon tea (or wine and cocktails) is served each day. *$69–$125. 1104 Montauk Ave., 36604, tel. 251/432–6440 or 800/938–6953, fax 251/433–4381, www.towle-house.com. 4 rooms. Complimentary breakfast, dining room, cable TV. AE, D, MC, V.*

MORE INFO

MOBILE AREA CONVENTION & VISITORS BUREAU ♦ *1 S. Water St., 36602, tel. 251/208–2000 or 800/566–2453, www.mobile.org.*

GETTING HERE

I–10 travels east from Mobile into Florida through Pensacola, west into Mississippi. I–65 slices Alabama in half vertically, passing through Birmingham and Montgomery and ending at Mobile.

MOBILE REGIONAL AIRPORT (tel. 251/633–0313, www.mobairport. com) is served by Delta, Northwest Airlink, Continental Express, and US Airways. It is about 7 mi west of I–65.

MONROEVILLE

Monroeville's most famous daughter, Harper Lee, won a Pulitzer Prize for her novel *To Kill a Mockingbird*, which incorporates many of her childhood remembrances of the small, inland town—and her friendship with novelist Truman Capote—in the 1930s. The local Monroeville Players offer the hottest theater tickets around with their amateur productions of a two-act play based on the book. Tickets for the May event sell out a few days after they go on sale in March.

SEE & DO

ALABAMA WRITERS' SYMPOSIUM ♦ In celebration of its status as the "literary capital of Alabama" (proclaimed by the Legislature in 1997), Monroeville hosts Alabama Southern Community College's annual symposium, a three-day literary festival, each May. *Tel. 251/575–3156, www.ascc.edu.*

✪ OLD COURTHOUSE MUSEUM Productions of *To Kill a Mockingbird* are staged at this museum, which was the model for the famous trial scene. The museum is open year-round; you can take a self-guided tour. *31 N. Alabama Ave., 36461, tel. 251/575–7433, www.tokillamockingbird.com.*

RIKARD'S MILL HISTORICAL PARK ♦ This is Alabama's only restored gristmill still standing on its original site and operational. There's also a covered bridge and blacksmith shop. *Rte. 265, Beatrice 36425, tel. 251/789–2781 or 251/575–7433, www.frontiernet. net/~mchm. $4. Apr.–mid-Dec., Thurs.–Sun. 11–dusk.*

MORE INFO

MONROEVILLE AREA CHAMBER OF COMMERCE ♦ *36 N. Alabama Ave., Monroeville 36460, tel. 251/743–2879, fax 251/743–2189, www.monroecountyal.com.*

GETTING HERE

Roughly halfway between Mobile and Montgomery, Monroeville is 25 mi north of I–65. Take the Monroeville exit from I–65 (Exit 93) onto U.S. 84 West, then at the intersection of U.S. 84 and CR 21, take CR 21 North into town.

BILOXI

Biloxi (pronounced bi-*lux*-i) is the oldest continuous settlement on the Gulf Coast and the third-largest city in Mississippi. When Pierre LeMoyne Sieur d'Iberville met the Native Americans who called themselves Biloxi, or "first people," he gave their name to the area and to the bay. The French constructed Fort Louis here; it served as the capital of the Louisiana Territory from 1720 until 1722, when the capital was moved to New Orleans. Today casinos bring the city plenty of action. Biloxi also has a number of museums and a white-sand beach for more sedate pursuits.

An odd amalgam of the old and new, Biloxi has a look and feel unlike any other city on the Gulf Coast. Here you'll find a sometimes bewildering mix of attractions: grand mansions in groves of moss-draped oaks, glitzy Las Vegas–style casinos, and tacky T-shirt shops, all vying for space along what the locals claim is the longest man-made beach in the world.

Since the founding of the Biloxi Colony by the French in 1699, five flags have flown over the city: French, Spanish, English, American, and Confederate. The population is diverse, with many residents of French, Italian, Scots-Irish, Slavic, and, more recently, Vietnamese descent.

Biloxi has had a long run as a beach resort—more than 150 years—and during that time it has weathered economic booms and busts. The city's economy is anchored primarily by the seafood industry and tourism. Many lavish summer homes line the beach, some built before the Civil War by Delta planters and wealthy families from New Orleans. Huge casino complexes now crowd the waterfront. Most of the city's attractions lie along or near Beach Boulevard, a thoroughfare lined with live oak and palm trees that can become congested during the summer tourist season. The Gulf Islands National Seashore lies a few miles offshore, offering pristine, sugar-white beaches in a wilderness setting. It's accessible only by boat.

Countless hurricanes have blown into Biloxi from the Gulf. The most notorious of these was Camille, which struck the city with 220-mph winds and a 30-foot storm surge in 1969. Biloxi residents have not been forced to evacuate in many years, but it's always a good idea to keep track of developing storms in summer and fall.

SEE & DO

BEAUVOIR, JEFFERSON DAVIS HOME & PRESIDENTIAL LIBRARY ♦ A National History Shrine, this is the last home and the presidential library of the President of the Confederacy, Jefferson Davis. *2244 Beach Blvd., tel. 228/388–9074, www.beauvoir. org. $7.50. Mar.–Oct., daily 9–5; Nov.–Feb., daily 9–4.*

BILOXI LIGHTHOUSE ♦ Erected in 1848, the 48-foot-tall lighthouse is a landmark. During the Civil War, Union forces, operating from Ship Island, blockaded Mississippi Sound and cut Biloxi off from much-needed supplies. When the Yankees demanded that Biloxi submit or starve, they were told that the Union would have to "blockade the mullet" first. Ever since, mullet has been known as "Biloxi bacon" and honored with its own festival each October. The city defended itself with what appeared to be a formidable cannon array near the lighthouse but was actually only two cannons and many logs painted black. *U.S. 90 at Porter Ave., tel. 228/435–6308. $2. Weekdays early morning only; call for hours, subject to change based on weather.*

CASINOS ♦ Most casinos listed here are inside hotels. All are open daily, 24 hours. There are no admission fees but you must be 21 years old or over to enter the gaming areas. **Beau Rivage Casino** (875 Beach Blvd., tel. 888/750–7111) is in the deluxe, grand Beau Rivage Hotel overlooking beach and bay. **Boomtown Biloxi Casino** (676 Bayview Ave., tel. 800/627–0777) is a Western-style casino located on Biloxi's beautiful back bay. **Casino Magic** (195 Beach Blvd., tel. 800/562–4425) is right on the Gulf and has a full-service hotel, nightly entertainment, and golf packages. **Grand Casino Biloxi** (265 Beach Blvd., tel. 800/946–2946) is a resort hotel and spa, as well as Biloxi's largest casino—with more than 2,800 slots and 80 gaming tables. **Imperial Palace Casino** (850 Bayview Ave., tel. 228/436–3000 or 800/436–3000) is modeled after the original casino in Las Vegas by the same name. Its elegant "Beauty-of-the-Orient"–inspired architecture graces the shores of Biloxi's back bay. **Isle of Capri Casino & Hotel** (151 Beach Blvd., tel. 800/843–4753) is a tropical paradise directly on the Gulf. It includes a 367-room hotel. The **Palace Casino** (158 Howard Ave., tel. 800/725–2239) is a floating palace of glass that offers table games, slots, and electronic games. **President Casino Broadwater Resort** (2110 Beach Blvd., tel. 800/843–7737), on the site of Biloxi's world-class Broadwater Resort, offers good dining and lodging, plus a full-service marina. **Treasure Bay Casino** (1980 Beach Blvd., tel. 800/747–2839, www.treasurebay.com) has an elaborate re-creation of a pirate ship, part of the complex's buccaneer theme.

CHURCH OF THE REDEEMER ♦ Only the 1894 bell tower remains of the original historic church, which was rebuilt after devastating Hurricane Camille. *610 Water St., tel. 228/436–3123. Free. Weekdays 9–3.*

J. L. SCOTT MARINE EDUCATION CENTER AND AQUARIUM ♦
The center has 48 live exhibits and aquariums brimming with reptiles and several species of fish from the Gulf. The centerpiece is a spectacular 42,000-gallon tank. *115 Beach Blvd., tel. 228/374–5550, fax 228/374–5550, www.aquarium.usm.edu. $5 ages 13–adult. Mon.–Sat. 9–4.*

MARDI GRAS MUSEUM ♦ Mardi Gras is almost as grand a celebration in Biloxi as in nearby New Orleans, and the Krewe costumes are equally festive. Costumes and crowns are housed in this museum in the old Magnolia Hotel, an 1847 structure listed on the National Register of Historic Places. *119 Rue Magnolia, tel. 228/435–6245. $2. Mon.–Sat. 11–4.*

✪ THE OHR-O'KEEFE MUSEUM OF ART Here you'll find a collection of intricate pottery crafted by the talented and eccentric George Ohr, known as "the mad potter of Biloxi." To truly appreciate his great craftsmanship, take a few minutes to watch the film about his life. The center also exhibits the work of local artists. A new addition, Pleasant Reed House, is a historical house built by former freed slave Pleasant Reed. Another center, designed by architect Frank Gehry to house the museum, is due to open in winter 2006. (The O'Keefe in the museum's name refers to a previous Mayor of Biloxi—also a major benefactor.) *136 G. E. Ohr St., tel. 228/374–5547, fax 228/436–3641, www.georgeohr.org. Museum or Pleasant Reed House $6; combination ticket $8. Winter, Mon.–Sat. 9–5; summer, Mon.–Sat. 9–6.*

OLD BRICK HOUSE ♦ This restored 1850s house, which serves as a community meeting center, combines American and French architectural elements. *622 Bayview Ave., tel. 228/435–6121, fax 228/435–6246. $2. Mon.–Sat. 11–4.*

POINT CADET PLAZA ♦ Across U.S. 90 is this waterfront complex that in the 1880s housed European immigrants who flocked to

Biloxi to work in seafood canneries. Exhibits at the **Maritime & Seafood Industry Museum** ($5, Mon.–Sat. 9–4:30) depict the growth and development of the Gulf Coast seafood industry. The museum contains historic photographs, exhibits, and artifacts relating to the Gulf Coast seafood industry. Two re-created schooners, which dock at Point Cadet's marina, are available for short trips and charters; call for fees. *Point Cadet Plaza, Hwy. 90 and 1st St., tel. 228/435–6320, fax 228/435–6309, www.maritimemuseum. org. Call for sailing times.*

SMALL CRAFT HARBOR ♦ Off U.S. 90 on the sound, this harbor feels like a sleepy fishing village. Take the **Biloxi Shrimping Trip** aboard the *Sailfish* and experience 70 minutes as a shrimper as you pull the nets through the waters. *Hwy. 90 and Main St., tel. 228/385–1182, www.gcww.com/sailfish. $12. Mar.–Nov.; call 1 wk in advance for public trips.*

✪ **TULLIS-TOLEDANO MANOR** Built by a New Orleans cotton and sugar broker in 1856, this Greek Revival antebellum house is now a historic museum. *360 Beach Blvd., tel. 228/435–6293. $2. Mon.–Sat. 11–4.*

VIEUX MARCHÉ WALKING TOUR ♦ This hour-long self-guided stroll through the heart of Old Biloxi is a virtual history lesson in Southern architecture. For a map and information on other recommended tours, contact the visitor center. *710 Beach Blvd., 39530, tel. 228/374–3105 or 800/245–6943, www.biloxi.ms.us. Free.*

EAT

CUCOS ♦ This attractive, casual restaurant two blocks north of the beach has Mexican art on its walls. The large open dining room is brought to life by margaritas, and beef and chicken fajitas. *$8–$12. 1851 Beach Blvd., 39531, tel. 228/388–1982. AE, D, DC, MC, V.*

THE FRENCH CONNECTION ♦ This restaurant, not far from Biloxi casino action, is known for its tar babies (boneless chicken cooked over pecan wood and wrapped with bacon, in a tarragon sauce). Four kinds of steak, plus smoked oysters, are also popular. There are three intimate dining areas—including one in an open court-yard with a fountain—with lace curtains, candlelight, and recorded piano music. *$18–$33. 1891 Pass Christian Rd., tel. 228/ 388–6367. AE, D, MC, V. Closed Sun. and Mon.*

HOOK, LINE, AND SINKER ♦ This veteran eatery is known for broiled stuffed flounder and its seafood platter. The walls are dec-orated with nautical items, and there's a view of the Gulf. *$10–$20. 2018 Beach Blvd., tel. 228/388–3757. AE, D, DC, MC, V. Closed Mon. and Dec. 17–27.*

✪ **MARY MAHONEY'S OLD FRENCH HOUSE RESTAURANT** Locals swear by it, not only for the comfort of its old brick and age-darkened wood (the mansion Mary Mahoney's calls home dates to 1737) and for the memory of Mary herself (who always went from table to table, chatting with customers), but also for the food. Start off with a bowl of rich, dark gumbo and move on to the lightly breaded panfried veal Antonio, topped with cheese sauce and plenty of fresh crabmeat for a main course. The bread pudding drenched in rum sauce is unforgettable. *$22–$44. 110 Rue Magnolia, tel. 228/374–0163, www.marymahoneys.com. AE, DC, MC, V. Closed Sun.*

MCELROY'S HARBOR HOUSE RESTAURANT ♦ Biloxi locals and real shrimpers eat hearty breakfasts, lunches, and dinners as shrimp boats come and go and fisherfolk load and unload their nets just outside. Notable are the po'boys, oysters on the half shell, broiled stuffed flounder, and stuffed crabs. *$15–$17. 695 Beach Blvd., tel. 228/435–5001. Reservations not accepted. AE, D, DC, MC, V.*

O'CHARLEY'S ♦ This restaurant is becoming one of the South's most notable. Pasta, seafood, and chicken are the most-popular

dishes, but there's also a broad choice of steaks and regional spe-
cialities. The outdoor dining area is covered and overlooks the
beach. There's a weekend brunch and kids' menu; kids eat free
every day here. *$10–$12. 2590 Beach Blvd., tel. 228/388–7883. AE,
D, DC, MC, V.*

OLE BILOXI SCHOONER ◆ Coast residents flock to this family-run
restaurant on Biloxi's serene back bay. It's tiny—little more than a
shack—but the food is good, especially the gumbo and the
po'boys, which come "dressed" and wrapped in paper. *$13–$15.
159 E. Howard Ave., by Palace Casino, tel. 228/374–8071. Reservations not accepted. No credit cards.*

SLEEP

✪ BEAU RIVAGE The first grand Las Vegas–style hotel-casino on
the Gulf Coast, Mirage resorts pulled out all the stops when it
built this impressive resort. In the lobby, majestic magnolia trees
line the inside walkway that leads from the entrance to the mega-
casino. The magnolia theme continues to the spacious modern
rooms where the Southern blooms decorate curtains and bedspreads. Among the 11 restaurants on the property, Porthouse is
the most spectacular, with floor-to-ceiling aquariums filled with
schools of fish. For entertainment, there's the 72,000-square-foot
casino with table games and slot machines. *$79–$269 rooms;
$199–$350 suites. 875 Beach Blvd., 39530, tel. 228/386–7444, 888/
567–6667 reservations, fax 228/386–7446, www.beaurivageresort.com.
1,460 rooms; 95 suites. 11 restaurants, café, ice cream parlor, room service, pool, health club, hair salon, hot tub, spa, dock, marina, bar, casino,
shops, no-smoking floors. AE, D, DC, MC, V.*

BILOXI BEACHFRONT HOTEL AT THE COLISEUM ◆ This motel 3
mi from downtown is made up of five low-rise buildings set
around a flower-planted courtyard in the center of the property.

$75–$90. 2400 Beach Blvd., 39531, tel. 228/388–3551 or 800/441–0882, fax 228/385–2032, www.biloxibeachfronthotel.com. 268 rooms. Restaurant, room service, in-room data ports, cable TV, pool, bar, laundry facilities, business services. AE, D, DC, MC, V.

BREAKERS INN ♦ This inn, 3 mi from downtown and opposite a sandy beach, has two-story condo-style rooms with full-service kitchens in town houses. There's free shuttle service to casinos. *$99–$150. 2506 Beach Blvd., 39531, tel. 228/388–6320 or 800/624–5031, fax 228/388–7185. 47 rooms. In-room data ports, kitchens, microwaves, refrigerators, cable TV, pool, wading pool, tennis court, laundry facilities, business services, some pets allowed. AE, D, MC, V.*

CASINO MAGIC BAY ST. LOUIS ♦ This 14-story hotel has elegant rooms, all with a view of the Gulf of Mexico. The Arnold Palmer–designed Bridges Golf Resort provides challenging action for novices and low-handicappers alike. There are slot machines and table games in the casino, and the entertainment complex showcases rock country bands and singers. A 100-site RV park on the premises ($23 plus tax) has barbecue grills. *$79–$99. 711 Casino Magic Dr., Bay St. Louis 39520, tel. 228/467–9257 or 800/562–4425, fax 228/469–2689, www.casinomagic-baystlouis.com. 291 rooms. 5 restaurants, room service, cable TV with movies, 18-hole golf course, pool, hot tub, spa, steam room, dock, 5 lounges, casino, laundry facilities, meeting rooms. AE, D, DC, MC, V.*

COMFORT INN ♦ This comfortable two-story hotel is across from a public beach and just a few miles from malls, casinos, and restaurants. Downtown is 3 mi west. *$119–$159. 1648 Beach Blvd., 39531, tel. 228/432–1993 or 800/228–5150, fax 228/432–2297, www.comfortinn.com. 68 rooms. Complimentary Continental breakfast, cable TV, pool, hot tub, business services. AE, D, DC, MC, V.*

EDGEWATER INN ♦ This three-story inn has two- and three-bedroom cottages with full kitchens, as well as regular rooms with ocean views and kitchen facilities. The property is across the street from a public beach and the casino strip, 3 mi west of downtown. *$69–$99 rooms; $139–$219 suites; $350–$395 cottages. 1936 Beach Blvd., 39531, tel. 228/388–1100 or 800/323–9676, fax 228/385–2406, www.gcww.com/edgewaterinn. 43 rooms; 19 suites; 4 cottages. Restaurant, in-room data ports, some kitchens, some kitchenettes, microwaves, refrigerators, cable TV, pool, exercise equipment. AE, D, DC, MC, V.*

✪ **FATHER RYAN HOUSE** This 1841 inn across from the Gulf (facing a public beach) is listed on the National Register of Historic Places. All rooms have views of theocean, gardens, or the courtyard and pool. Rooms are furnished with handcrafted beds and early-19th-century antiques. Rooms have access to an upstairs terrace. The house is named for Father Abram Ryan, Poet Laureate of the Confederacy. *$100–$130 rooms; $165–$175 suites. 1196 Beach Blvd., 39530, tel. 228/435–1189 or 800/295–1189, fax 228/436–3063, www.frryan.com. 10 rooms; 5 suites. Complimentary breakfast, in-room data ports, some in-room hot tubs, cable TV, pool. AE, D, DC, MC, V.*

GRAND CASINO BILOXI HOTEL AND BAYVIEW RESORT & SPA ♦ These two Grand Casino properties are across the highway from each other on U.S. 90 and are connected by a climate-controlled, covered walkway. Together they offer 1,000 comfortable, bright, and airy rooms. There's also a teen arcade. The 1,800-seat Biloxi Grand Theatre here hosts live stage shows. Adjacent is the Grand Casino, with Las Vegas–style gambling. Hotel guests are shuttled to and from the property's Jack Nicklaus–designed, Grand Bear championship golf course. *$109–$249 rooms; $189–$329 suites. 265 Beach Blvd., 39530, tel. 228/436–2946 or 800/354–2450, www.grandbiloxi.com. 915 rooms; 85 suites. 13 restaurants, 18-hole golf course, 2 pools, gym, hair salon, spa, 6 bars, 2 lounges, shops, casino, children's programs (ages 6 wks–12 yrs), concierge, car rental, travel services, free parking. AE, D, DC, MC, V.*

GREEN OAKS BED & BREAKFAST ♦ Mississippi's oldest antebellum mansion, built in the 1820s, occupies 2 acres and a private beach. The three-story house is listed on the National Register of Historic Places, and is furnished with hardwood floors and fine antiques, including Oriental rugs and four-poster beds. Breakfast and afternoon tea are included. *$140–$150. 580 Beach Blvd., 39530, tel. 228/436–6257 or 888/436–6257, fax 228/436–6225, www.gcww. com/greenoaks. 5 rooms. Complimentary breakfast, in-room data ports, cable TV, beach. AE, D, DC, MC, V.*

ISLE OF CAPRI CASINO CROWNE PLAZA RESORT ♦ The Isle of Capri was the first gaming operation to open on the Gulf. Rooms are large, with ceiling fans; some have balconies with views of the Gulf. The casino, with slot machines, video poker, and table games, can be accessed through the mezzanine level. Weekends are usually packed here, so you might want to call ahead. *$119–$139. 151 Beach Blvd., 39530, tel. 228/435–5400 or 800/843–4753, fax 228/436–7804, www.isleofcapricasinos.com. 370 rooms. 3 restaurants, pool, health club, casino, meeting rooms. AE, D, DC, MC, V.*

PALACE CASINO RESORT ♦ Standard rooms overlook Biloxi Bay and the Gulf of Mexico. The soaring atrium lobby has a 25-foot skylight and a cascading fountain that marks the entrance to the casino. Outside, elegant cabanas ring the pool and are adjacent to a beach area (but there's no water access right here, you have to walk to the water, nearby). *$79–$119 rooms; $500–$1,500 suites. 158 Howard Ave., 39530, tel. 228/432–8888 or 800/725–2239, fax 228/386–2300, www.palacecasinoresort.com. 236 rooms; 11 suites. 3 restaurants, café, in-room data ports, golf privileges, putting green, pool, gym, hair salon, outdoor hot tub, massage, sauna, spa, marina, volleyball, 2 bars, 2 lounges, casino, theater, shop, laundry service, concierge, concierge floor, airport shuttle, free parking. AE, D, DC, MC, V.*

PRESIDENT CASINO BROADWATER RESORT ♦ This 1970s resort 5 mi west of downtown offers many recreational options: it faces white-sand beaches, has a golf course, and runs deep-sea fishing excursions from its marina. There's a free shuttle to the

President Casino, which is part of the complex. Many of the clientele are retirees. The complex includes an eight-story building, two- and three-bedroom cottages, and motel-style buildings. *$60–$89; cottages $300. 2110 Beach Blvd., 39531, tel. 228/385–3500 or 800/843–7737, fax 228/385–4102, www.presidentbroadwater.com. 491 rooms; 9 cottages. 3 restaurants, some kitchenettes, some refrigerators, cable TV, 3 pools, 18-hole golf course, 10 tennis courts, gym, boating, marina, fishing, basketball, volleyball, 2 bars, playground. AE, D, DC, MC, V.*

QUALITY INN EMERALD BEACH ♦ This older two-story motel, 5 mi west of downtown, sits on its own sandy gulf beach. *$89–$149. 1865 Beach Blvd., 39531, tel. 228/388–3212 or 800/342–7519, fax 228/388–6541, www.qiemeraldbeachbiloxi.com. 71 rooms. Complimentary Continental breakfast, in-room data ports, microwaves, refrigerators, cable TV, pool, beach, business services. AE, D, DC, MC, V.*

THE SANTINI–STEWART HOUSE BED & BREAKFAST ♦ This 1837 cottage, across the street from the beach, is on the National Register of Historic Places. It was also the last home of confederate general Alexander P. Stewart. Innkeepers James and Patricia Dunay serve wine and cheese afternoons in the garden. You can spend evenings in front of the fireplace, surrounded by Louis XIV furnishings. There are four rooms in the main cottage, and a separate honeymoon cottage. *$75–$125; $125–$150 honeymoon cottage. 964 Beach Blvd., 39530, tel. 228/436–4078 or 800/686–1146, fax 228/432–9193, www.santinibnb.com. 4 rooms; 1 cottage. Complimentary breakfast, in-room data ports, cable TV, hot tub, beach, bicycles. AE, D, MC, V.*

TREASURE BAY CASINO RESORT ♦ This nine-story resort hotel has a casino—inside a 400-foot replica of an 18th-century pirate ship—that's built to resemble a fort. The beach is across the street. Some rooms have views of the casino/pirate ship, and the Gulf. The hotel garden has a two-tier swimming pool with waterfalls.

Legend has it that buccaneers roamed the area in the 1700s. *$69–$99 rooms; $179 suites. 1980 W. Beach Blvd., 39531, tel. 228/ 385–6000, fax 228/385–6067, www.treasurebay.com. 252 rooms; 6 suites. 4 restaurants, in-room data ports, some kitchenettes, refrigerators, some in-room hot tubs, cable TV, golf privileges, 2 pools, wading pool, hair salon, massage, beach, bar, casino, business services. AE, D, MC, V.*

MORE INFO

The Biloxi Chamber of Commerce *1048 Beach Blvd., Biloxi 39530, tel. 228/374–2717, www.biloxi.org.* **The Biloxi Visitors Center** *710 Beach Blvd., Biloxi 39530, tel. 228/374–3105 or 800/245– 6943, www.biloxi.ms.us.* **Mississippi Gulf Coast Convention and Visitors Bureau** *942 Beach Blvd., Gulfport 39507, tel. 228/896–6699 or 888/467–4853, www.gulfcoast.org.*

GETTING HERE

Biloxi is just south of I–10; take I–10 to U.S. 90 to reach the casinos and the beach.

GULFPORT-BILOXI INTERNATIONAL AIRPORT ♦ (Airport Rd. off Washington Ave., Gulfport, tel. 228/863–5951) is served by AirTran, ASA–The Delta Connection, Continental Express, Northwest Airlink, and Southeast and Southeast Vacation (a tour operator service for Southeast).

GULFPORT

A sister city to the tourist resort of Biloxi, Gulfport has the feel of a truly southern small town. It offers some of the Gulf Coast's best restaurants and cultural experiences, along with one "grand" casino and a beautiful yacht club and small craft harbor.

As Mississippi's largest seaport, Gulfport is more working town than tourist resort. But as a coastal city—particularly one less than an hour from rowdy New Orleans—it's a place where people know how to enjoy life.

Gulfport is a fairly young city by Gulf Coast standards, since most of its early growth came during the railroad boom in the late 19th century. But owing to its location and massive investments, it quickly surpassed every other port between New Orleans and Mobile. It's still growing by leaps and bounds, thanks to increasing shipping, booming casino development, and frenzied construction in the I–10/U.S. 49 interchange area. Not surprisingly, there are growing pains: traffic in particular has become a problem. But once you reach Beach Boulevard (U.S. 90), you'll be treated to a panorama view of the Gulf of Mexico; and some of the most beautiful homes on the coast are concentrated along the city's eastern beaches.

There are also several nearby nature areas, including the Gulf Islands National Seashore, the De Soto National Forest, and scenic Wolf River.

SEE & DO

CASINOS ♦ All casinos have free admission and are open 24 hours. **Copa Casino** (777 Copa Blvd., tel. 800/946–2672) is in a permanently docked, 500-foot cruise ship. **Grand Casino Gulfport** (3215 W. Beach Blvd., tel. 800/946–7777) is in the Oasis Resort and Spa. They offer activities for people under 21.

CEC/SEABEE MUSEUM ♦ This museum is dedicated to the U.S. Navy's Civilian Engineer Corps (CEC). You can learn the history of the CEC and the Seabees through exhibited photographs and documents. *5200 2nd St., tel. 228/871–3164. Free. Weekdays 9–5, Sat. 9–5.*

DE SOTO NATIONAL FOREST ♦ The 500,487 acres of this national forest cover the southeast corner of the state, south from Laurel to the Gulf of Mexico, a few miles inland from Gulfport. The area includes Airey Lake, Big Biloxi Recreation Area, Big Foot Horse Trail, and the Tuxachanie National Recreation Trail. You can hunt, canoe, hike, and camp on the grounds. *654 W. Frontage Rd., Wiggins 39577, tel. 601/928–4422. Free. Daily.*

🐾 **FUNTIME USA** ♦ With its playground, bumper boats, and cars, and more than 100 arcade games, this amusement park provides hours of entertainment for children of all ages. *U.S. 90 and Cowan Rd., tel. 228/896–7315. Grounds free; 75¢–$3 for rides and games. June–Aug., daily 9 AM–midnight; Sept.–May, daily 9 AM–10 PM.*

GRASS LAWN ♦ This stately beachfront mansion was built in 1836 with wooden-peg construction and pine and cypress from nearby forests. The upper and lower galleries face the sea. *720 E. Beach Blvd., tel. 228/868–5907. Free. Tues.–Thurs. 9–11 AM and 1:30–3:30 PM.*

🐾 **MARINE LIFE OCEANARIUM** ♦ In the small craft harbor in the Joseph T. Jones Memorial Park are shows with performing dolphins, sea lions, and macaws. *Joseph T. Jones Memorial Park, east* *of intersection of U.S. 49 and U.S. 90, tel. 228/863–0651. $13.75. July–Sept., daily 9–6; Oct.–June, daily 9–3. Call for hours, which are subject to change.*

SHOP

Prime Outlets of Gulfport (Exit 34A off I–10, 10000 Factory Shops Blvd., tel. 228/867–6100) has more than 80 famous-brand shops offering factory-outlet prices. The shops are connected by a covered walkway. A food court, tourist information booth, and playground are also on the premises.

OUTDOORS

✪ **Gulf Islands National Seashore.** Pristine Gulf Islands National Seashore is one of the hidden treasures of the Gulf Coast. The Mississippi portion (the park boundary extends to Florida) consists of five barrier islands about 10 mi off the coast and a small enclave of bayous on the mainland. The shores are almost wholly undisturbed by development. Indeed, the two larger islands, Horn and Petit Bois, are federally designated wilderness areas. The surf pounds hard on the island beaches—unlike those on the mainland, where waves seldom exceed a foot or two—because the islands are separated from the mainland by the shallow Mississippi Sound.

Reaching the islands can be a challenge. Passenger ferries run from Gulfport to West Ship Island, but the other islands are accessible only by private boat. The islands can also be inhospitable. There are hordes of mosquitoes and biting "no-see-ums," and there's little or no shelter from storms or the relentless summer sun. Finally, there's always a chance of encountering sharks or alligators.

For privacy and natural solitude, however, the islands can't be beat. Except for sunny weekends in summer and fall, it's possible to walk half a day here without encountering another human being. You can share an afternoon swim with none but a family of curious dolphins. The sand is sugar white, dunes rise as high as 30 feet, and the water is clear with a blue-green tint. Wildlife—particularly bird life—is abundant.

The islands can be pleasant in any season, but the best time to visit is in spring and fall, when temperatures are generally moderate. Storms are common any time of year, but particularly during hurricane season, which lasts from August to November. With the exception of West Ship, visitors must pack their own food and water, and the only available lodging is primitive camping. **Davis Bayou Area,** on the mainland near Ocean Springs, consists of 400 acres of salt marsh, bayous, and maritime forests. You can camp, fish, picnic, and hike scenic trails. You'll find a tent area, picnic shelters, a boat launch, and self-guided nature trails. There's no beach access. *Park Rd. off U.S. 90, tel. 228/875–9057. Free. Daily.*

Gulf Shore Islands. West Ship is the only one of these beautiful islands accessible by passenger ferry. The others can be reached by charter or private boat. East Ship Island was severed from West Ship Island when Hurricane Camille passed through in 1969. It's uninhabited and undeveloped; you can swim, fish, and camp. Portions of Cat Island were recently incorporated into the boundaries of Gulf Islands National Seashore. It offers primitive camping, uninhabited beaches, and solitude. Thirteen miles long and about ¾ mi at its widest point, Horn Island is the largest and probably the most scenic of the Gulf islands. It has natural beaches, tall sand dunes, subtropical forests, and inland lagoons. There's a ranger station on Horn Island (though staff members may not always be present), and primitive camping is allowed. Painter Walter Anderson of Ocean Springs once tied himself to a pine tree on the island to experience the full force of a hurricane.

Petit Bois Island, about 7 mi long, is the easternmost of the islands. It's the most remote and has the least vegetation—and the fewest visitors. Primitive camping is allowed. West Ship Island has the only real facilities—snack bar, covered picnic pavilions, and bathhouse—and is the only island where most visitors simply come for a day on the beach. Camping is not allowed. Fort Massachusetts is on West Ship, and can be toured. It's an impressive brick structure built in response to the War of 1812 to prevent foreign invasion of New Orleans. During the Civil War, the island was used by the U.S. Navy as a base of operations for the coastal blockade. **Gulf Islands National Seashore Visitors Center.** At Davis Bayou in Ocean Springs, the center offers exhibits, nature trails, campgrounds, ranger programs, showers, a boat launch, and picnic areas. The bayou and surrounding woodlands are one of the last unspoiled areas on the coast. *3500 Park Rd., Ocean Springs, tel. 228/875–9057. Free. Daily 8:30–sunset.*

Licensed Charter Boats. The only way to reach Cat, East Ship, Horn, and Petit Bois Islands is by taking a licensed charter boat. Call the Gulf Islands National Seashore Visitor Center for the list of charters that are legally permitted to go to the islands. *Tel. 228/875–9057 Gulf Islands National Seashore Visitor Center.*

Mid-South Sailing and Charters (tel. 228/863–6969, www.midsouthsailing.com, $35 per person, Daily 9 AM–dusk) offers sailboat cruises at the Gulfport Small Craft Harbor.

✪ **Ship Island Excursions.** You catch the ferry to West Ship here at the Gulfport Small Craft Harbor, which is at the end of Highway 49 S. If you don't have time for a stroll on the island, you can take a turnaround cruise. *Hwy. 49 S, Gulfport, tel. 228/864–1014 or 866/466–7386, www.msshipisland.com. $20 round-trip. Departures Mar.–mid-May and Sept. and Oct., weekdays 9, weekends 9 and noon; mid-May–Aug., weekdays 9 and noon, weekends 9, 10:30, 12, 2:30.*

If you have time for only one activity on this part of the coast, make it a getaway to **West Ship Island** on the passenger ferry from the **Gulfport Small Craft Harbor.** The ferry runs once a day, at 9, on weekdays, and twice on weekends Mar.–mid-May and Sept.–Oct. (9 and noon). It runs more frequently on weekends in summer—mid-May–Aug., weekdays 9 and noon, and weekends 9, 10:30, 12, and 2:30. The trip takes about 60 minutes. At West Ship Island, a part of Gulf Islands National Seashore, a U.S. park ranger will guide you through **Fort Massachusetts,** built between 1859 and 1866. The rangers will treat you to tales of the island's colorful Civil War past. West Ship Island was used as a Union supply depot, ship repair facility, POW camp, and staging area for local skirmishes and battles, such as the Battles of New Orleans and Mobile Bay. Spend the day sunning, swimming in the clear green water, and beachcombing for treasures washed up by the surf. *Ticket office at Gulfport Harbor in Joseph T. Jones Memorial Park, east of intersection of U.S. 49 and U.S. 90, tel. 228/864–1014 or 866/466–7386. Ferry $20. Ferry runs Mar.–Oct.*

Wolf River Canoe Canoe and Kayak (21640 Tucker Rd., tel. 228/452–7666, $36 per canoe, $25 per kayak) rents canoes and provides shuttle services for trips on the scenic Wolf River. Full-day tours commence at 9 and are available on the hour; the latest you can leave on a half-day trip is 2.

EAT

✪ **CHAPPY'S** Special-occasion dining for Gulf Coast residents often means a visit to this pleasant restaurant in Long Beach, just a few miles from Gulfport. Specialties include rich gumbo, redfish panfried Cajun style, and barbecue shrimp. The fish, fresh from the Gulf, is cooked by chef Chappy himself. *$15–$29. 624 E. Beach Blvd., Long Beach, tel. 228/865–9755, www.chappys.net. AE, D, DC, MC, V.*

✪ **THE CHIMNEYS** After establishing itself at the Long Beach Harbor as a favorite lunch and dinner place for locals and visitors alike, this restaurant relocated to Gulfport—to a gracious turn-of-the-20th-century Queen Anne–style home with a stunning view of the Gulf. The kitchen serves up trout dishes, shrimp prepared a variety of ways, and blackened fillet of fish stuffed with a savory blend of crabmeat and shrimp. *$20–$25. 1640 E. Beach Blvd., Gulfport, tel. 228/868–7020, www.chimneysrestaurant.com. AE, D, DC, MC, V. Closed Mon.*

✪ **VRAZEL'S FINE FOOD** The interior of this charming brick building has a soothing intimacy about it, with soft lighting and dining nooks with large windows facing the beach or overlooking exquisite gardens. Choose from a substantial list of coastal water fare: red snapper, Gulf trout, flounder, and shrimp prepared every which way. When amberjack is the special, it's a sure hit. *$22–$25. 3206 W. Beach Blvd. (U.S. 90), Gulfport, tel. 228/863–2229, www.vrazels.com. AE, D, DC, MC, V. Closed Sun. No lunch Sat.*

SLEEP

BEST WESTERN BEACH VIEW INN ♦ This motel is across from the Grand Casino and the Copa Casino, two blocks from the Marine Life Oceanarium, and 2 mi southwest of downtown. *$69–$90. 2922 W. Beach Blvd., 39501, tel. 228/864–4650 or 800/748–8969, fax 228/863–6867, www.bestwestern.com. 150 rooms. Complimentary Continental breakfast, cable TV, pool, laundry facilities. AE, D, DC, MC, V.*

✪ **GRAND CASINO GULFPORT HOTEL & OASIS RESORT & SPA** These two hotels are on either side of U.S. 90. They're connected by a covered, climate-control walkway. Although accommodations are in two separate buildings, the amenities and restaurants are easily accessible from both properties. Rooms are basic and comfortable; however, the ones at the Oasis have a slightly more laid-back, beachy feel. Kids Quest day care keeps the little ones entertained, and there's a shuttle to the property's Grand Bear golf course. You'll find that 24-hour casino action is never more than a few steps away. *$89–$259 rooms; $179–$399 suites. 3215 W. Beach Blvd., Gulfport 39501, tel. 228/870–7777 or 800/354–2450, www. grandcasinos.com. 940 rooms; 60 suites. 6 restaurants, room service, in-room data ports, 5 pools, gym, hair salon, spa, bar, casino, children's programs (ages 6 wks–12 yrs), concierge, car rental. AE, D, DC, MC, V.*

GULF ISLANDS NATIONAL SEASHORE VISITORS CENTER ♦
This campsite offers RV facilities for $16 per night. The site has showers, hookups, a dump station, and electricity. Four islands, which can be reached by boat charter, offer primitive camping. Be sure to bring about a gallon of water per person for every day you'll be camping. *$16. 3500 Park Rd., Ocean Springs 39564, tel. 228/875–9057, www.nps.gov/guis. 51 campsites. MC, V.*

HOLIDAY INN BEACHFRONT ♦ This complex of low-rise beachfront buildings was built in 1979. *$79–$120. 1600 E. Beach Blvd., 39501, tel. 228/864–4310 or 800/441–0887, fax 228/865–0525, www.holiday-inn.com. 227 rooms. Restaurant, room service, in-room data ports, cable TV, pool, wading pool, bar, laundry facilities. AE, D, DC, MC, V.*

RED CREEK INN, VINEYARD & RACING STABLE ♦ This three-story B&B was built in 1899 in a raised French cottage style, with a 64-foot front porch. The 4-acre grounds are filled with fragrant magnolias and ancient live oak trees. There are also a vineyard and a racing stable (but no riding). Rooms are individually named and decorated in different period styles. Red Creek, 4 mi west of Gulfport, was the first B&B on the Gulf Coast. The breakfast here is relatively elaborate—an extensive, sit-down affair. *$65–$137. 7416 Red Creek Rd., Long Beach 39560, tel. 228/452–3080 or 800/ 729–9670, www.redcreekinn.com. 5 rooms. Complimentary Continental breakfast; no room phones, business services, no smoking. No credit cards.*

MORE INFO

Gulf Islands National Seashore *3500 Park Rd., Ocean Springs 39564, tel. 228/875–9057.* **Mississippi Gulf Coast Convention and Visitors Bureau** *942 Beach Blvd., Gulfport 39507, tel. 228/896–6699 or 888/467–4853, www.gulfcoast.org.*

GETTING HERE

To get to Gulfport, take I–10 from east or west, then take Highway 49 South to Highway 90 which runs parallel to the Gulf of Mexico.

GULFPORT-BILOXI INTERNATIONAL AIRPORT ♦ (Airport Rd. off U.S. 49, Gulfport, tel. 228/863–5951) is served by AirTran, ASA–The Delta Connection, Continental Express, Northwest Airlink, and Southeast and Southeast Vacation (a tour operator service for Southeast).

OCEAN SPRINGS

To begin at the beginning, at least as far as Mississippi is concerned, start in Ocean Springs. Here, in 1699, the French commander Pierre LeMoyne Sieur d'Iberville established Fort Maurepas to shore up France's claim to the central part of North America. This first colony was temporary, but it's fondly remembered by Ocean Springs during its annual spring festival on the first weekend in April, which celebrates Iberville's landing. Magnificent oaks shade the sleepy town center, a pleasant area of small shops to explore on foot.

Don't be misled by the four-lane commercial sprawl along U.S. 90—Ocean Springs is, along with Bay St. Louis, the closest you'll come to the quaint villages once common along the Mississippi Coast. A small enclave of tree-shaded streets, many with views of the Mississippi Sound, the town has a local feel, which is all the more remarkable given the comparatively touristy areas farther west and the heavily industrial areas to the east.

The town's main claim to fame is Shearwater Pottery, a family artists' compound that nurtured the eccentric and gifted Walter Anderson, whose works can be seen in the nearby Community Center and in the art museum that bears his name. Ocean Springs is also home to the headquarters of the Gulf Islands National

Seashore Visitor Center. And just 5 mi northeast of the city, along I–10, is the Mississippi Sandhill Crane National Wildlife Refuge.

SEE & DO

🕯 **DOLL HOUSE** ♦ The Doll House displays a collection of contemporary and antique dolls, stuffed animals, and dollhouses. *1201 Bienville Blvd. (U.S. 90), tel. 228/872–3971. $1 donation requested for YMCA. Mon.–Sat. 1–5.*

✪ **MISSISSIPPI SANDHILL CRANE NATIONAL WILDLIFE REFUGE** This refuge is a safe haven for approximately 120 of the tall endangered cranes. Tours to view the cranes are offered in January and February. There are 10 species of carnivorous plants in the refuge, and a ¾ mi nature trail through savannah and bayou areas. The refuge is 5 mi northeast of Ocean Springs. *7200 Crane La., Gautier 39553, tel. 228/497–6322, mississippisandhillcrane.fws.gov. Free. Weekdays 7:30–4.*

OCEAN SPRINGS WALKING & DRIVING TOUR ♦ A brochure from the Ocean Springs Chamber of Commerce will guide you on a walking and driving tour of the trail, shaded by moss-draped trees and bordered by weathered but lovely summer houses. The route, which begins at Ocean Springs's train station, winds through the area first explored 300 years ago by Pierre LeMoyne Sieur d'Iberville.

✪ **WALTER ANDERSON MUSEUM OF ART** An artist of genius and grand eccentricity, Walter Anderson (1903–65), made his home in Ocean Springs. Drawings and watercolors, some not discovered until after his death, are on display at the museum, built as an attachment to the **Old Community Center** where Anderson painted murals in 1951 (before it became the "Old" Community Center). The **Little Room** was extracted from Anderson's cottage home, loaded on a flatbed truck, and moved to the museum, with its murals intact. Anderson painted the intricate murals in the Old Community Center for a fee of $1; they are now appraised at $1 million. *510 Washington Ave., tel. 228/872–3164, www.walterandersonmuseum.org. $6. May–Sept., Mon.–Sat. 9:30–5, Sun. 12:30–5; Oct.–Apr., Mon.–Sat. 9:30–4:30, Sun. 12:30–4:30.*

✪ **SHEARWATER POTTERY AND SHOWROOM** A wide selection of original Anderson family hand-thrown and hand-cast pottery is displayed here. Potters demonstrate their craft in the Anderson family workshop; some pieces are for sale. This was also the original site of Anderson's cottage, since moved to the Walter Anderson Museum of Art. Prints made from Anderson's fanciful block prints are for sale here. *102 Shearwater Dr., tel. 228/875–7320. Free. Showroom Mon.–Sat. 9–5:30, Sun. 1–5:30; workshop weekdays 9–noon, 1–4.*

SHOP

At **Ballard's Pewter** (1110 Government St., Ocean Springs, tel. 228/875–7550) you'll find necklaces and earrings made from sand dollars—or you can have the pewterer make a bespoke (custom-made) piece.

At **Realizations** (1000 Washington Ave., in the old Train Depot, tel. 228/875–0503) you can buy Walter Anderson prints and clothing printed with his unique designs.

EAT

GERMAINE'S ♦ Formerly Trilby's, this little house surrounded by live oaks has served many a great meal to its faithful clientele. It's reminiscent of New Orleans, with unadorned wooden floors, walls decked in local art for sale, fireplaces, and attentive service. Specialties include crabmeat au gratin, broiled trout served with mushrooms and sautéed crabmeat, and sautéed veal in a creamy port wine sauce. *$13–$25. 1203 Bienville Blvd., U.S. 90 E, tel. 228/875–4426. AE, D, MC, V. Closed Mon. No dinner Sun.*

✪ **JOCELYN'S RESTAURANT** This is as good as Gulf Coast seafood gets. Specialties are fresh crabmeat fixed three or four ways. Trout, flounder, and, when available, snapper are subtly seasoned and served with garnishes as bright and original as modern art. *$15–$21. U.S. 90 E, opposite South Trust Bank, tel. 228/875–1925. Reservations not accepted. No credit cards. No lunch. Closed Sun.–Tues.*

SLEEP

DAYS INN OF OCEAN SPRINGS ♦ Several local casinos run shuttles right to the door of this budget motel, which is a 10-minute drive from the Gulf of Mexico. *$50–$110. 7305 Washington Ave., 39564, tel. 228/872–8255, fax 228/872–8210, www.daysinn.com. 65 rooms. In-room data ports, some microwaves, some refrigerators, some in-room hot tubs, outdoor pool, some pets allowed. AE, D, DC, MC, V.*

INDIAN HEAD SUPER 8 MOTEL ♦ This two-story budget chain motel is close to casinos, restaurants, golf, the beaches, and fishing. *$59–$99. 500 Bienville Blvd., 39564, tel. 228/872–1888, fax 228/875–8750. 60 rooms. Complimentary Continental breakfast, in-room data ports, cable TV, laundry facilities, business services. AE, D, MC, V.*

MORE INFO

OCEAN SPRINGS CHAMBER OF COMMERCE MAIN STREET VISITOR CENTER ♦ *1000 Washington Ave., Ocean Springs 39564, tel. 228/875–4424, www.oceanspringschamber.com.*

GETTING HERE

From the Gulfport Airport, take I–10 east to Exit 50, then south to Ocean Springs. Ocean Springs is 15 mi east of Gulfport airport.

GULFPORT-BILOXI INTERNATIONAL AIRPORT ♦ (Airport Rd. off U.S. 49, Gulfport, tel. 228/863–5951) is served by AirTran, ASA–The Delta Connection, Continental Express, Northwest Airlink, and Southeast and Southeast Vacation (a tour operator service for Southeast).

PASS CHRISTIAN

With sailboats plying the Gulf, and waterfront mansions framed by magnificent live oak trees, Pass Christian comes as close to the idealized vision of a Gulf Coast city as any in Mississippi. Free of the sprawl of casinos, fast-food restaurants, and T-shirt shops, it's largely residential and, as a result, noticeably more quiet and sedate. Still, it's just a short drive (relatively—it's 65 mi) from New Orleans, the casinos of Bay St. Louis, and the tourist areas of Gulfport and Biloxi. Pass Christian's unusual name comes from the fact that it is located near the pass (a narrow waterway) that leads into the Bay of St. Louis.

Sailboat racing in the South began here, and consequently the second yacht club in the country was formed in this town (it still exists today)—Louisiana landowner Zachary Taylor was at the yacht club when he was persuaded to run for the presidency.

Twenty-six miles of man-made beach extend from Biloxi to Pass Christian. Toward the west the beaches become less commercialized and less crowded; Pass Christian's is the best of all. Tan, sail, jet ski, beachcomb, or swim—there are no waves, and the ocean here is good for families.

On Pass Christian's scenic drive, which runs parallel to U.S. 90, is some of the most admired real estate in the country. Most homes on the scenic drive are on the National Register of Historic Places, and you can tour many of them during the annual home tour (on the first Sunday in May) of the **Pass Christian Historical Society** (tel. 228/452–0063).

SEE & DO

✪ **THE FRIENDSHIP OAK** Legend has it that if you walk with someone in the shade of the huge 500-year-old Friendship Oak on the Gulf Coast campus of the University of Southern Mississippi, you will remain friends forever. *730 E. Beach Blvd., Long Beach 39560, tel. 228/865–4573, fax 228/867–2658, www.usm. edu. Free.*

SHOP

Hillyer House (207 E. Scenic Dr., tel. 228/452–4810, www. hillyerhouse.com, AE, D, MC, V) sells handmade jewelry, pottery, glass, and brass made by local and regional artists, plus packaged Southern delicacies.

EAT

ANNIE'S ♦ You can eat your meal sitting in copper booths at this Southern cottage. There's a glass-roof patio decorated with flowers, plantation bells, iron pots, a fireplace used in winter, and a fountain that gushes in summer. Kids go for chicken fingers, adults enjoy broiled flounder and fried chicken plates. *$10–$20. 120 W. Bayview St., 39571, tel. 228/452–2062. AE, D, MC, V. Closed Dec. and Mon. and Tues.*

MORE INFO

PASS CHRISTIAN CHAMBER OF COMMERCE ♦ *Corner of Hwy. 90 and West Harbor, Pass Christian 39571, tel. 228/452–2252.*

GETTING HERE

To get to Pass Christian, take I–10 from east or west, then Highway 49 south at the Gulfport exit. Take Highway 49 to Highway 90, which runs parallel to the Gulf of Mexico. Take Highway 90 west to Pass Christian, 7 mi from Gulfport.

Less than 10 mi away from Pass Christian is the **Gulfport-Biloxi International Airport** (Airport Rd. off U.S. 49, Gulfport, tel. 228/863–5951, www.gulfcoast.org/gpt), which is served by Air Tran, ASA–The Delta Connection, Continental Express, Northwest Airlink, and Southeast and Southeast Vacation (a tour operator service for Southeast).

Louis Armstrong New Orleans International Airport (900 Airline Dr., Kenner, LA 70062, tel. 504/464–0831, www.flymsy.com) is about 75 mi from Pass Christian.

PASCAGOULA

Pascagoula is primarily a center for heavy industry and ship-building, and it looks the part. Giant cranes line the waterfront, and refineries and fish-rendering plants tower above the outlying marshes. The water is murky, of course, so you won't be inclined to swim.

On the Gulf in the southeastern corner of the state, Pascagoula has been a significant port since the early 1800s, when the river was dredged. The volume of cotton and lumber production up-river led the city to deepen and widen the channel again in the 1870s. More changes took place after the Jackson County Port Authority was established in 1956.

Now, only the shrimp boats and a few old homes hint at Pascagoula's former life as a quiet coastal town. But you don't have to pass up Pascagoula. Of interest are three nature areas, two museums, and several scenic neighborhoods along the waterfront. Northrop Grumman Ship Systems, south of the Pascagoula River bridge on U.S. 90, is impressive, too. And then there's the river itself, which sometimes emits an unusual high-pitched buzz.

SEE & DO

GULF COAST GATOR RANCH ♦ Walk along boardwalks above alligators basking in the sun, or take a tour and a boat ride. You can also see beavers and other animals. *10300 U.S. 90, Pascagoula 39563, tel. 866/954–2867, 228/475–6026, or 228/475–6643, www.gatorranch. com. Air boat ride $20; walk $5. Mon.–Sat. 9–5, Sun. 9–5 (airboat starts at noon).*

LONGFELLOW HOUSE ♦ This place was once rumored to have been visited by American poet Henry Wadsworth Longfellow (1807–82); thus the name. (He didn't actually visit, however, though he mentioned "Pascagoula's sunny bay" in his poem, "The Building of the Ship.") The house, which was built in 1850, is not open to the public. *3401 Beach Blvd., tel. 228/762–9611.*

LOWER PASCAGOULA RIVER WILDLIFE MANAGEMENT AREA ♦ This remote labyrinth of freshwater swamps offers hunting, fishing, boating, hiking, and primitive camping. It's one of the last remaining stands of old-growth forest in the region, and quite spectacular. The Pascagoula River Wildlife Management Area, north of town, includes some of the few surviving old-growth swamp forests on the Gulf Coast. *816 Wade-Vancleave Rd., Moss Point 39562, tel. 228/588–3878, fax 228/588–6248. Free.*

OLD SPANISH FORT MUSEUM ♦ This is not really a fort—it's a house—and it's not really Spanish—it's French. The La Pointe-Krebs House, as it's sometimes called, *is* the oldest private building in the Mississippi Valley. The house was built in 1718 with cypress and juniper, and chinked with a mix of clay, moss, and a plaster made of ground oyster shells. The adjacent museum displays 18th-century objects and Native American artifacts. There's also a hands-on exhibit for kids. *4602 Fort St., 39567, tel. 228/769–1505, fax 228/769–1432. $4. Tues.–Sat. 9:30–4:30.*

SCRANTON NATURE CENTER AND SCRANTON MUSEUM ◆
The Scranton Nature Center is a museum about sea and land life, and exhibits about fossils, minerals, and animals. A separate museum 5 mi away, housed in part on a 70-foot-long retired shrimp boat in River Park, has a preserved deck, galley, bunkroom, and wheelhouse—and on its lower level, a wetlands diorama and three large aquariums. It also has a playground. *Nature Center, I. G. Levy Park N; Scranton Museum, River Park on U.S. 90, east of town near the high-rise bridge, 39581, tel. 228/938–6612, fax 228/938–6795. Free. Tues.–Sat. 10–4, Sun. 1–4.*

SHEPARD STATE PARK ◆ You can canoe, camp, bike, and hike along nature trails at this park 3 mi west of town and south of U.S. 90. *1034 Graveline Rd., Gautier 39553, tel. 228/497–2244, fax 228/497–3468. $2 per vehicle. Daily 8 AM–8 PM.*

EAT

TIKI RESTAURANT, LOUNGE, AND MARINA ◆ A variety of seafood dishes and steaks—including a 10-ounce blackened prime rib and red snapper cones—can be enjoyed inside or on two decks over the water at this restaurant on the bayou. There's karaoke all week and a band performs weekends. The restaurant is 3 mi west of Pascagoula. *$10–$16. 3212 Mary Walker Dr., Gautier 39553, tel. 228/497–1591, fax 228/497–1575. AE, D, DC, MC, V.*

SLEEP

DAYS INN MOSS POINT ◆ This two-story motel is 8 mi from the Gulf of Mexico and 6 mi from downtown. The '90s stucco building is near several excellent restaurants. *$60. 6700 Hwy. 63, Moss*

Point 39563, tel. 228/475–0077 or 800/325–2525, fax 228/475–3783, www.daysinn.com. 54 rooms. Complimentary Continental breakfast, microwaves, refrigerators, cable TV, pool. AE, D, DC, MC, V.

LA FONT INN RESORT ♦ This 1963 two-story brick hotel 5 mi from downtown has a distinctive glass-and-metal pyramid. It's on 9 acres of landscaped grounds, and is minutes away from casinos, beaches, fishing, and golf courses. *$69. 2703 Denny Ave., Pascagoula 39568-1028, tel. 228/762–7111 or 866/647–6077, 800/821–3668 within MS, fax 228/934–4324, www.lafontinn.com. 192 rooms. Restaurant, room service, bar, in-room data ports, some kitchenettes, refrigerators, cable TV, 2 tennis courts, pool, wading pool, exercise equipment, hot tub, sauna, playground, laundry facilities, business services, some pets allowed. AE, D, DC, MC, V.*

MORE INFO

JACKSON COUNTY CHAMBER OF COMMERCE ♦ *720 Krebs Ave., Pascagoula 39568-0480, tel. 228/762–3391, www.jcchamber.com.*

GETTING HERE

From the Gulfport Airport, take I–10 east to Highway 63, then south on Highway 63 to U.S. 90, then west on U.S. 90 to Pascagoula. Pascagoula is 32 mi east of Gulfport airport.

WAVELAND

Waveland and neighboring Bay St. Louis share a nearly indistinguishable border, and, wonderfully, have somehow managed to retain their small town coastal charm. Both are popular weekend destinations for city dwellers, and nearby Buccaneer State Park can get crowded during the summer months.

Waveland, incorporated in 1888, is a young coastal town. It suffered major damage during Hurricane Camille in 1969, and there are still many vacant lots where houses were washed or blown away. Its main thoroughfare, busy U.S. 90, is full of fast food chains and major discount stores.

Bay St. Louis, which dates to 1818, is surrounded by the Mississippi Sound and St. Louis Bay. It's the more attractive of the bordering towns. More than 100 buildings here are listed in the National Register of Historic Places, and the movie *This Property is Condemned,* based on a Tennessee Williams play, was filmed in the depot district downtown. The area north of the city is predominately rural, aside from the upscale residential development called Diamondhead, which is just off I–10, and NASA's Stennis Space Center, the only free NASA tour in the country.

SEE & DO

BUCCANEER STATE PARK ◆ This park has an Olympic-size wave pool, open from Memorial Day through Labor Day, that may lure you from the nature trail, the beach, and picnic sites. There are 129 campsites in a grove of live oaks streaming with moss. The park, open year-round, also has two tennis courts with lights, two basketball courts, and a seasonal camp store. *1150 S. Beach Blvd., tel. 228/467–3822. Wave pool daily 11–6:30. Park admission $2 per vehicle, up to 4 people, plus 50¢ extra per additional person. Wave pool $9 adult, $7.50 children under 12.*

CASINO MAGIC ◆ The casino in the Casino Magic Inn offers all the usual table and video games. *711 Casino Magic Dr., Bay St. Louis 39520, tel. 800/562–4425. Free. Daily 24 hours.*

HANCOCK COUNTY WELCOME CENTER ◆ Travelers who think of Waveland as just a spot to get onto I–10 for New Orleans are missing one of the most accessible tourist information offices on the Gulf Coast. *I–10 Exit 2, at Hwy. 607, tel. 228/533–5554.*

✪ **HISTORIC DOWNTOWN WALKING TOUR OF OLD BAY ST. LOUIS** This self-guided tour of town includes numerous antiques shops and historic buildings. *Tel. 800/466–9048.*

✪ ☾ **NASA STENNISPHERE SPACE CENTER** This visitor center at the Stennis Space Center has a 14,000-square-foot museum, a mock space-shuttle cockpit, a flight simulator, and a mock of a tech center where engineers test engines and shoot modules to the moon. The motion simulator sends you on a five-minute trip to Mars. There's also a model of an international space station, plus a gift shop, a restaurant, and a rocket park that includes an F1 engine (one of only five of these engines, which took the Saturn 5 crew to the moon). *Exit 2 off I–10, Stennis Space Center 39529, tel. 228/688–2370 or 800/237–1821. Free; motion simulator $5, www. ssc.nasa.gov. Daily 9–3.*

R. BARTHE SCULPTURE ♦ The Hancock Public Library displays work by native sculptor Richmond Barthe, whose internationally acclaimed *Woman's Head* was the subject of an exhibition at the Smithsonian Institution's Anacostia Museum in 1993. *333 Coleman Ave., Waveland 39520, tel. 228/467–5282, fax 228/467–5503, www.hancock.lib.ms.us. Free. Mon. 9–6:30, Tues.–Fri. 9–6, Sat. 9–4.*

ST. AUGUSTINE SEMINARY AND GROTTO ♦ This is the state's oldest seminary for the training of African-American Roman Catholics for the priesthood. There's also a new retreat center here. *199 Seminary Dr., Bay St. Louis 39520, tel. 228/467–6414, 228/467–9837 retreat center, fax 228/466–4393. Free. Daily anytime.*

EAT

LIL RAY'S ♦ Though the appointments are limited to trestle tables and benches, this is a place to dream about when you're hungry for seafood platters and po'boys. A waitress, asked by a customer for a diet drink, said it best: "Mister, this ain't no diet place." *$6–$10. 613 Hwy. 90, tel. 228/467–4566. Reservations not accepted. D, MC, V.*

SLEEP

CASINO MAGIC INN ♦ This four-story Gulf-front hotel and casino complex has an 18-hole golf course designed by Arnold Palmer, and an RV Park. The Magic Casino is across the street. *$59–$79. 711 Casino Magic Dr., Bay St. Louis 39520, tel. 228/466–0891 or 800/562–4425, fax 228/467–7900, www.casinomagic-baystlouis.com. 201 rooms. 5 restaurants, some refrigerators, cable TV, pool, marina, casino, laundry facilities. AE, D, DC, MC, V.*

MORE INFO

MISSISSIPPI'S WEST COAST, HANCOCK COUNTY ♦ *408A U.S. 90, Bay St. Louis 39520, tel. 800/466–9048, fax 228/463–9227, www. hancockcountyms.org.*

GETTING HERE

Take I–10 from east or west to Exit 2 or Exit 13 south to Highway 90. Bay St. Louis is approximately 40 mi east of New Orleans and 20 mi west of Gulfport.

GULFPORT-BILOXI INTERNATIONAL AIRPORT ♦ (Airport Rd. off U.S. 49, Gulfport, tel. 228/863–5951) is served by AirTran, ASA–The Delta Connection, Continental Express, Northwest Airlink, and Southeast and Southeast Vacation (a tour operator service for Southeast).

LOUIS ARMSTRONG NEW ORLEANS INTERNATIONAL AIRPORT ♦ (900 Airline Dr., Kenner, LA 70062, tel. 504/464–0831, www.flymsy.com).

WIGGINS

Wiggins is known as the home of baseball great Dizzy Dean. It's also a good base for exploring some of the finest remaining natural areas in the Deep South. Within a short distance in almost any direction from Wiggins are broad expanses of botanically diverse forests, including hilly lands crossed by clear streams, and wild, almost impenetrable swamps. The area's history is tied to the timber industry and the landscape around the town remains largely wooded. Wildlife is abundant and the rivers and streams are almost pristine. There are two federally designated wilderness areas, and numerous state wildlife management areas with plenty of opportunities for hunting, fishing, and wildlife-watching.

SEE & DO

ASHE LAKE ♦ You can hike on nature trails, camp, and fish—no swimming, though—at this lake north of Wiggins via U.S. 49. From Brooklyn take Ashe Nursery Road south to Highway 308 and continue south ¼ mi. *Hwy. 308, Brooklyn, tel. 601/928–4422. Free. Daily.*

BATSON'S LOG HOME AND FISH FARM ♦ The farm offers camping on Red Creek, fishing in clear, spring-fed ponds, and log-cabin and nature-trail tours. *1802 U.S. 26, tel. 601/928–5271 fishing and tours. $5 per person (min. 12 people). By appointment.*

DE SOTO NATIONAL FOREST ♦ Ten miles north of Wiggins is the largest national forest in the state, covering half a million acres. The primarily piney woods forest includes Black Creek Wilderness—a 5,025-acre area along the banks of Black Creek (a federally designated Wild and Scenic River) known for its lush foliage and typically southern Mississippi topography. You can take scenic float and canoe trips, swim, camp, and hike up to 40 mi alongside Black Creek. (Canoe rentals are available.) You can also attempt one of Mississippi's most challenging hikes, the Black Creek Trail, which has 40 mi of difficult hiking, 10 mi in the Black Creek Wilderness. Or try another: for more than 30 mi, the Big Foot Horse Trail System has a rider's camp, parking, and camping, but no potable water. Tuxachanie Trail has almost 23 mi for hiking. Bethel ATV Trail is for those who like to do their exploring on motorized vehicles; there's also camping. The Frontage Road office has trail maps. **Red Creek** (U.S. 49, Perkinston 39573, tel. 601/928–4422, free), a lazy creek 5 mi north of Wiggins, flows through terrain that ranges from hilly pine forests to cypress swamps. The name is accurate: the water has a reddish-brown hue that comes from tannic acid in decaying leaves. There is also a privately run RV park and campground called Perk Beach (☎601/928–9111). *654 W. Frontage Rd., Wiggins, tel. 601/928–4422. Free. Daily dawn–dusk.*

FLINT CREEK WATER PARK ♦ Just about 2 mi north of town, off Highway 29, this park offers camping, cabins, fishing, swimming, and nature trails. *1216 Parkway Dr., tel. 601/928–3051, www.phwd. net. $1.25. Daily 7 AM–8 PM.*

OUTDOORS

For information on boating, contact **Black Creek Canoe Rental** *20 Old Hwy. 49W, Brooklyn 39425, tel. 601/582–8817, www.*

blackcreekcanoe.com. $18–$50. Mar.–Oct., daily; Nov.–Feb., by reserva-
tion only.

MORE INFO

STONE COUNTY ECONOMIC DEVELOPMENT PARTNERSHIP ♦
311 Court St., Box 569, Wiggins 39577, tel. 601/928–5418, www.
stonecounty.com.

GETTING HERE

Wiggins is 30 mi north of I–10 (at Gulfport), right off U.S. 49—
where 49 intersects with east–west Route 26.

GULFPORT-BILOXI INTERNATIONAL AIRPORT ♦ (Airport Rd.
off U.S. 49, Gulfport, tel. 228/863–5951) is served by AirTran,
ASA–The Delta Connection, Continental Express, Northwest
Airlink, and Southeast and Southeast Vacation (a tour operator
service for Southeast).

APALACHICOLA

Apalachicola—meaning "land of the friendly people" in the language of its original Native American inhabitants and known in these parts as simply Apalach—lies on the Panhandle's southernmost bulge. Settlers began arriving in 1821, and by 1847 the southern terminus of the Apalachicola River steamboat route was a bustling port town. Although the town is now known as the Oyster Capital of the World, oystering became king only after the local cotton industry flagged—the city's extrawide streets, built to accommodate bales of cotton awaiting transport, are a remnant of that trade—and the sponge industry moved down the coast after depleting local sponge colonies. But the newest industry here is tourism, and visitors have begun discovering the Forgotten Coast, as the area is known, flocking to its intimate hotels and B&Bs, dining at excellent restaurants, and browsing through unique shops selling everything from handmade furniture to brass fixtures recovered from nearby shipwrecks. If you like oysters or you want to go back in time to the Old South of Gothic churches and spooky graveyards, Apalachicola is a good place to start.

Drive by the **Raney House,** circa 1850, and **Trinity Episcopal Church,** built from prefabricated parts in 1838. The town is at a developmental turning point of late, pulled in one direction by well-intentioned locals who want to preserve Apalachicola's port-town roots and in the other by long-time business owners who fear preservation will inhibit commercial growth. For now, however, the city exudes a refreshing authenticity—think Key West in the early 1960s—that many others in the Sunshine State lost long ago, one that might be lost to Panama City Beach–style overdevelopment unless local government institutes an official historic preservation committee.

SEE & DO

APALACHICOLA HISTORIC DISTRICT ♦ You'll find fine examples of antebellum architecture in the historic section of Apalachicola. The largest concentration of historic homes is in the area south of Avenue E (Highway 98), between 7th and Market streets. You can pick up a free walking tour map at the Chamber of Commerce during business hours. *99 Market St. #100, 32320, tel. 850/653–9419, fax 850/653–8219, www.apalachicolabay.org. Free. Weekdays 9–5.*

APALACHICOLA NATIONAL ESTUARINE RESEARCH RESERVE ♦ These 193,659 acres of land and water include two barrier islands, the lower 52 mi of the Apalachicola River, and the Apalachicola Bay system. The reserve's visitor and education center is in the Robert L. Howell building in Apalachicola, which also runs public exhibits, lectures, education programs, and has an adjoining nature trail. *261 7th St., tel. 850/653–8063, fax 850/653–2297. Free. Daily; visitor center weekdays 8–5.*

APALACHICOLA NATIONAL FOREST ♦ The largest of Florida's three national forests, Apalachicola National Forest covers 565,000 acres of hardwood hammocks, pine flatwoods, lakes, and rivers. The Florida National Scenic Trail runs 73 mi through the forest. There's also an 8½-mi mountain bike trail and a 31-mi horse trail. Camping, fishing, swimming, and canoeing are all popular. The park spreads north of town and west of Tallahassee and U.S. 319. *57 Taff Dr., Crawfordville 32327, tel. 850/926–3561. Free. Daily 24 hrs.*

FORT GADSDEN HISTORIC SITE ♦ Fort Gadsden is a requisite tour for Civil War buffs. Built by the British as a base to recruit Native Americans and African-Americans during the War of 1812, the fort was abandoned in 1815 until used as a supply resource by the Confederate Army. It's in the Apalachicola National Forest in a town called Sumatra; follow signs from Highway 65. *Hwy. 20 S, Bristol, tel. 850/926–3561 or 850/643–2282. Free. Daily 9–5.*

JOHN GORRIE MUSEUM STATE PARK ♦ The museum honors the physician credited with inventing ice making and, almost, air-conditioning. Although he was hampered by technology, later air-conditioning patents utilized Gorrie's discoveries. Exhibits of Apalachicola history are displayed here as well. *Ave. D and 6th St., tel. 850/653–9347. $1. Thurs.–Mon. 9–5.*

ST. GEORGE ISLAND STATE PARK ♦ The park occupies 1,962 acres, with 9 mi of undeveloped beaches, dunes, salt marshes, and pine and oak forests. You can camp and hike on 2½ mi of trails, which have observation platforms for bird-watching. The park is on 29-mi-long St. George Island, a 20-minute drive across the Apalachicola Bay from town. It's home to many of the area's top beach vacation accommodations, though these are primarily rental homes. *1900 E. Gulf Beach Dr., St. George Island 32328, tel. 850/927–2111, fax 850/927–2500, www.baynavigator.com. Free; state park $4 per vehicle. Daily 8 AM–dusk.*

✪ ST. JOSEPH PENINSULA STATE PARK This pristine 2,516-acre park in Port St. Joe has 20 mi of bay and Gulf beaches, but is most famous for its bird-watching. More than 200 species have been spotted within the park, and the area is the top spot in the eastern U.S. for observing hawks during their fall migration. There are 119 campsites, luxury furnished bayside cabins, saltwater fishing, boating, canoeing, hiking on two ½–1 mi trails, and seasonal ranger programs. *8899 Cape San Blas Rd., Port St. Joe 32456, tel. 850/227–1327, fax 850/227–1488, www.dep.state.fl.us/parks. $3.25 per vehicle. Daily 8 AM–dusk.*

ST. VINCENT ISLAND NATIONAL WILDLIFE REFUGE ♦ Once private, this 12,358-acre barrier island off the coast of Apalachicola has a unique blend of native and exotic wildlife. Asian Sambar deer coexist with indigenous white-tailed deer, and the island has a population of American bald eagles. The fauna and 14 mi of beach attract day-trippers. Note that the park is accessible only by boat, but the visitor center in Apalachicola can put you in touch with a private tour operator to arrange transportation. The visitor center is located in Apalachicola's John B. Meyer Harbor House. *Visitors Center: 479 Market St., Apalachicola 32329, tel. 850/653–8808. Weekdays 8–4:30.*

SHOP

Avenue E (15 Ave. E, Apalachicola, tel. 850/653–1411) is a stylish store that specializes in reasonably priced antique and reproduction pieces, including furniture, lamps, artwork, and interior accessories. The **Grady Market** (76 Water St., Apalachicola, tel. 850/653–4099) is a collection of more than a dozen boutiques, including several antiques dealers and the gallery of Richard Bickel, known for his stunning black-and-white photographs of local residents. The **Tin Shed** (170 Water St., Apalachicola, tel. 850/653–3635) has an impressive collection of antiques and knickknacks, from antique brass luggage tags to 1940s-era nautical charts to sponge-diver wetsuits to hand-glazed tiles and architectural elements salvaged from demolished buildings.

EAT

BLUE PARROT ♦ You can order just about any seafood dish under the gaze of the hanging fish on the walls. Fresh grouper, crab cakes, or the surf and turf are house specialties to be enjoyed either downstairs or on the upstairs patio overlooking the Gulf of Mexico. At night the connected tiki bar livens up the neighborhood. *$10–$21. 65 W. Gorrie Dr., 32328, tel. 850/927–2987. AE, D, MC, V.*

BOSS OYSTER ♦ Eat your oysters fried, Rockefeller-style, or on the half shell at this laid-back eatery overlooking the Apalachicola River. Eat 'em alfresco at picnic tables or inside in the busy, rustic dining room, but don't let the modest surroundings fool you—oysters aren't cheap here or anywhere in town. If you're allergic to seafood, don't worry—the menu also includes staples, such as steak and pizza. *$10–$24. 123 Water St., tel. 850/653–9364. AE, D, DC, MC, V.*

CAROLINE'S DINING ON THE RIVER ♦ This restaurant has great views on the Apalachicola River. You can eat indoors on the patio. There is also a regularly scheduled band upstairs. The seafood is great and includes such selections as shrimp, grouper, shrimp, scallops, and oysters. *$15–$25. 123 Water St., 32320, tel. 850/653–8139. AE, D, DC, MC, V.*

GIBSON INN ♦ This inn's somewhat formal dining room—with polished wooden floors and white tablecloths—is a great place to stop in for breakfast, lunch, or dinner, even if you're not a guest. The chef cooks seafood, steak, pasta, salad, and dessert with vigor. Stuffed grouper Florentine or veal scaloppine served over fettucine are big hits, along with rib-eye steak stuffed with portobello mushrooms and topped with crabmeat. *$17–$26. 51 Ave. C, Apalachicola 32320, tel. 850/653–2191, fax 850/653–3521. AE, MC, V. Closed Mon. and Tues.*

MAGNOLIA GRILL ♦ Chef-owner Eddie Cass has earned local and regional acclaim from food critics who have discovered the culinary pearl in this small oyster town. Such dishes as Magnolia Grill Surf and Turf, which weds oak-grilled pork tenderloin with béarnaise sauce to jumbo shrimp with New England crabmeat stuffing and lobster sauce, pleasingly unite the flavors of Eddie's native New England and the coastal South. Dinners here tend to be leisurely events, and the stellar desserts—anything chocolate will wow you—deserve an hour of their own. *$15–$30. 99 11th St., tel. 850/653–8000. Reservations essential. MC, V. Closed Sun. No lunch.*

NOLA'S GRILL ♦ Hobnob with Apalachicola aristocracy as you eat in a serene, Edwardian-style dining room at the town's traditional hotel. The place is a bit formal—crisp, creased linen tablecloths and atmospheric lighting—and the food is impeccable. The menu changes seasonally, but count on fresh seafood, namely oyster, shrimp, and grouper preparations. Even if you've eaten dinner elsewhere, make sure to stop by the cozy wooden bar for an after-dinner drink and a taste of the Apalachicola of yesteryear. *$16–$28. 51 Ave. C, tel. 850/653–2191. AE, MC, V.*

OWL CAFÉ ♦ This old-fashioned, lovely lunch and dinner spot has a dining room defined by white-linen elegance, and a colorful garden terrace. The menu is artful: Grandma's chicken sandwich with potato salad seems as much at home on the lunch menu as the crab and shrimp quesadillas. Dinner seafood specials are carefully prepared, but special requests are sometimes met with resistance from the kitchen. Fine wines for adults and special menu selections for children make this a family-friendly place. *$8–$15. 15 Ave. D, tel. 850/653–9888. AE, MC, V. Closed Sun.*

✪ **TAMARA'S CAFE FLORIDITA** Tamara, a native Venezuelan, brings the food and warmth of her homeland to this colorful bistro, which mixes Florida flavors with South American flair. For starters, try the creamy black bean soup or the pleasantly spicy oyster stew; for dinner choose from grouper paella, prosciutto-wrapped salmon with mango-cilantro sauce, or margarita chicken and scallops with a tequila-lime glaze. All entrées come with black beans and rice, fresh vegetables, and focaccia bread, but if you still have room for dessert try the fried banana split or the *tres leches,* a South American favorite. The chef, who keeps watch over the dining room from an open kitchen, is happy to accommodate a whim. *$16–$21. 17 Ave. E, tel. 850/653–4111. AE, MC, V.*

SLEEP

BEST WESTERN APALACH INN ◆ Basic but impeccably kept, this modern property 1 mi from the downtown waterfront area has everything you need. Standard guest rooms are done in earth tones with wicker headboards and burgundy-print curtains and bedspreads. A large swimming pool and free local calls are unexpected bonuses. *$65–$78. 249 U.S. 98 W, 32320, tel. 850/653–9131, fax 850/653–9136, www.bwapalachinn.com. 42 rooms. Complimentary Continental breakfast, in-room data ports, cable TV, pool. AE, D, MC, V. CP.*

COOMBS HOUSE INN ◆ Nine fireplaces and an ornate oak staircase with lead-glass windows on the landing lend authenticity to this restored 1905 mansion. No two guest rooms are alike, but all are appointed with Victorian-era settees, four-poster or sleigh beds, English chintz curtains, and Asian rugs on polished hardwood floors. A full breakfast is served in the dining room. Eighty steps away is Coombs House East, and, beyond that, a renovated carriage house. Popular for weddings and receptions, these may be the most elegant homes in Apalachicola. Free tours are offered in the afternoon if the accommodations are not in use. *$89–$225. 80 6th St., 32320, tel. 850/653–9199, fax 850/653–2785, www.coombshouseinn. com. 18 rooms. Dining room, cable TV, bicycles. D, MC, V.*

✪ **THE CONSULATE** These four elegant suites, on the second story of the former offices of the local French Consul, range in size from 600 to 1,600 square feet, and combine a 19th-century feel with 21st-century luxury. Exposed wooden beams and brick walls, 13-foot ceilings, hardwood floors, and antique appointments add more than a hint of charm, while custom-built kitchens, full-size washers and dryers, and cordless room phones make living easy. The two front units share an expansive balcony, where you can take in the constant parade of fishing vessels headed out the Intracoastal. The homelike amenities make this a popular spot for families, larger groups, and even wedding parties, and discounts are given for stays longer than two nights. The Grady Market, a locally owned art and clothing boutique, occupies the building's first floor. *$175–$290. 76 Water St., 32320, tel. 850/653–1515 or 877/239–1159, www.consulatesuites.com. 4 suites. Kitchens, cable TV, in-room VCRs. AE, MC, V.*

✪ **GIBSON INN** One of a few inns on the National Register of Historic Places still operating as a full-service facility, this turn-of-the-20th-century hostelry in the heart of downtown is easily identified by its wraparound porches, fretwork, and captain's watch. Rooms are furnished with period pieces, such as four-poster beds, antique armoires, and pedestal lavatories, which have wide basins and porcelain fixtures. *$100–$105, $115–$140 suites. 57 Market St., 32320, tel. 850/653–2191, fax 850/653–3521, www.gibsoninn.com. 30 rooms; 2 suites. Restaurant, bar, cable TV, some pets allowed. AE, MC, V.*

RANCHO INN ♦ This mom-and-pop operation—the owners live on-site—prides itself on its homeyness and personalized service. Rooms are spotless, if a little dated in their beige-and-brown color schemes, but 25-inch color TVs (complete with HBO and other premium channels) and in-room coffeemakers and other amenities make it a hard-to-beat option for those on a budget. *$85 (more for holiday weekends or special events), $10 extra per person for suites.*

240 U.S. 98 W, 32320, tel. 850/653–9435, fax 850/653–9180, www. ranchoinn.com. 31 rooms, 1 suite. Microwaves, refrigerators, cable TV, pool. AE, D, DC, MC, V.

MORE INFO

APALACHICOLA BAY CHAMBER OF COMMERCE ♦ *128 Market St., Apalachicola 32320, tel. 850/653–9419, www.baynavigator.com.*

GETTING HERE

Apalachicola is on U.S. Highway 98, 65 mi southeast of Panama City Beach. To get here from I–10, the main inland thoroughfare, take State Road 65 south to the coast then head west 10 mi on Highway 98 to the Apalachicola Bay Bridge. The city is on the west side of the bridge.

BLOUNTSTOWN

Blountstown (population 2,500), the seat of Calhoun County, lies midway between the Georgia border and the Gulf of Mexico, 50 mi west of Tallahassee in the Panhandle. From Blountstown, you have easy access to the Apalachicola National Forest, a 600,000-acre, wildlife-rich woodland park crossed by canoe trails and footpaths. Blountstown was named after John Blount, a Seminole Indian Chief who, as a guide for General Andrew Jackson, aided in the 1818 invasion of Spanish Florida. Blount visited President Jackson in Washington, D.C., and was rewarded with a reservation on the west side of the Apalachicola River. A restored 1903 courthouse downtown is a registered Florida landmark.

SEE & DO

TORREYA STATE PARK ♦ Nineteen miles from Blountstown, this park offers camping, picnic spots, and a number of excellent nature trails. The Apalachicola River Bluffs Trail runs along the river past Confederate gun pits, bluffs, and hardwood forests. The Weeping Ridge Trail heads through one of the park's deep ravines. Rangers offer tours of the 1849 Gregory House and tell stories of river's-edge plantation life. *Hwy. 1641, tel. 850/643–2674. $2 per vehicle. Daily 8–dusk.*

EAT

PARRAMORE'S RESTAURANT TOO ♦ This restaurant, which has wooden tables and booths, is the follow-up to the popular restaurant half an hour away in Sneads. The fried catfish and T-bone steak are among diners' favorites. *$8–$14. 16438 Chipola Rd., 32424, tel. 850/674–3400. No credit cards. Closed Sun.*

SLEEP

AIRPORT MOTEL ♦ Blountstown's only motel, named for the now-defunct local airport, sits quietly in the countryside. *$35–$40. Hwy. 20 E, 32424, tel. 850/674–8168. 30 rooms. Cable TV. AE, D, DC, MC, V.*

MORE INFO

CALHOUN COUNTY CHAMBER OF COMMERCE ♦ *20816 Central Ave. E, #2, Blountstown 32424, tel. 850/674–4519, fax 850/674–4962, www.calhounco.org.*

GETTING HERE

Take State Road 69 south off I–10, 50 mi west of Tallahassee. Continue south about 20 mi to Blountstown, which is at the intersection of State Road 20.

CHATTAHOOCHEE

On a high bluff overlooking the Apalachicola River and Lake Seminole on the Georgia border, this one-time Federal Arsenal during the Civil War has great fishing, boating, camping, and water sports. The lush rolling woodlands at one of Florida's highest elevations, bisected by I–10, 12 mi west of Tallahassee, make the town (population 3,913) popular with bikers. Nearby Lake Seminole is a huge lake (37,500 acres) with 500 mi of shoreline. Gadsden County's North Florida Art Trail follows roadways to art galleries, artists' studios, historic tobacco barns, bed-and-breakfast inns, bright outdoor murals, Victorian homes, and historic landmarks from Chattahoochee into surrounding towns.

The town's name is said to be from the Cherokee word for colored or marked stone. In 1819 General Andrew Jackson came to the area to establish civil government in northern Florida. In the early 1900s the area became known as River Junction and was incorporated in 1921, becoming Chattahoochee in 1938.

EAT

THE HOMEPLACE RESTAURANT ♦ Football plaques and early 1900s advertising signs decorate this restaurant, known for juicy hamburgers, fried chicken, and steaks. *$6–$9. 415 W. Washington St., 32324, tel. 850/663–4040. No credit cards.*

SLEEP

ADMIRAL BENBOW MORGAN LODGE ♦ This single-story lodge off Highway 90 has a 24-hour restaurant next door. Lake Seminole is just minutes away. *$50–$55. 116 E. Washington St., 32324, tel. 850/663–4336 or 800/451–1986, fax 850/663–4336, www.admiralbenbow.com. 43 rooms. Some microwaves, some refrigerators, cable TV, some pets allowed (fee). AE, D, MC, V.*

MORE INFO

SOUTHWEST QUARTER CHATTAHOOCHEE CHAMBER OF COMMERCE ♦ *201 N. Lumpkin St., Cuthbert, GA 31740, tel. 912/732–2683, fax 912/732–6590.*

GETTING HERE

Chattahoochee lies 12 mi west of Tallahassee directly on I–10.

CHIPLEY

This Panhandle town of 4,100 on I–10, at the intersections of State Highways 77 and 90, is named for magnate William D. Chipley, who in the late 19th century created one of the first major railroads in Florida, then went on to become a state senator. A plaque in front of the agricultural center on I–90 west reads KUDZU DEVELOPED HERE, in honor of Lillie and C. E. Pleas, locals who spent three decades developing and promoting the fast-growing vine.

Chipley, the seat of Washington County, is 50 mi inland from the Gulf of Mexico, near the state's northern border. Two miles south on Highway 77 is Falling Waters State Recreation Area, famous for Falling Waters Sink, a waterfall visible from an observation deck. Ten miles northeast of Falling Waters (take U.S. 231 off I–10) is Florida Caverns State Park, which, besides stalactites and stalagmites, has canoeing and campsites on the Chipola River. You can also canoe, dive, and swim in Cypress Springs, a huge spring 15 mi south of Chipley in Vernon.

SEE & DO

✪ **FALLING WATERS STATE PARK** This site of a Civil War–era whiskey distillery and, later, an exotic plant nursery—some imported species still thrive in the wild—is best known for being the site of one of Florida's most notable geological features—the Falling Waters Sink. The 100-foot-deep cylindrical pit provides the background for a waterfall, and there's an observation deck for viewing this natural phenomenon. The water free-falls 67 feet to the bottom of the sink, but where it goes after that is a mystery. You can hike the numerous short trails to see the many sink holes, a swimming lake, and a butterfly garden. *1130 State Park Rd., off Rte. 77 A, 32428, tel. 850/638–6130, fax 850/638–6273, www.floridastateparks.org/fallingwaters. $3.25 per vehicle up to 8 people. Daily 8–dusk.*

FLORIDA CAVERNS STATE PARK ♦ Take a ranger-led cave tour to see stalactites, stalagmites, and "waterfalls" of solid rock at this expansive park. Some of the caverns are off-limits to the public or open for scientific study only with a permit, but you'll still see enough to fill a half day or more. Between Memorial Day and Labor Day, rangers offer guided lantern tours on Friday and Saturday nights. There are also hiking trails, campsites, and areas for swimming and canoeing on the Chipola River. *3345 Caverns Rd., off U.S. 90 on S.R. 166, Marianna 32446, tel. 850/482–9598, www. floridastateparks.org/floridacavern. $3.25 per vehicle up to 8 people. Daily 8–dusk.*

SLEEP

HOLIDAY INN EXPRESS ♦ This motel is about 3 mi east of downtown Chipley. *$80, $90 suites. 1700 A Main St., 32428, tel. 850/638–3996 or 800/465–4329, fax 850/638–4569, www.hiexpress.com. 48 rooms; 2 suites. In-room data ports, refrigerators, some in-room hot tubs, cable TV, outdoor pool, business services, some pets allowed (fee). AE, D, DC, MC, V.*

MORE INFO

CHIPLEY CITY HALL ♦ *1442 Jackson Ave., Chipley 32428, tel. 850/638–6350, www.cityofchipley.com.*

WASHINGTON COUNTY CHAMBER OF COMMERCE ♦ *685 7th St., Chipley 32428, tel. 850/638–4157, fax 850/638–8770, www.washcomall.com.*

GETTING HERE

Chipley is about 85 mi west of Tallahassee off I–10, at the intersection of state highways 77 and 90. Fifty miles due south of Chipley via State Road 77 is the vacation mecca of Panama City Beach and the Gulf Beaches.

CRESTVIEW

One of the highest towns in Florida is at the junction of I–10 and U.S. 90 and State Road 85 (at 235 feet above sea level, residents say they're "on top of the mountain"). The town was a crossroads as far back as the Old Spanish Trail, when conquistadors passed through on trade routes.

Today, Crestview is one of the fastest-growing towns in northwest Florida. Its population has more than doubled since 1990, to 50,000. Much of that population is related to the three Air Force bases outside of town. Eglin Air Force Base, with 724 square mi of land, is the largest military installation in the Western Hemisphere.

SEE & DO

✪ **BLACKWATER RIVER STATE FOREST** The largest state forest in Florida, about 15 mi northwest of Crestview, has more than 190,000 acres of pine, oak, dogwood, and cedar trees. Three scenic rivers—the Blackwater, Shoal, and Yellow rivers—course through the forest, and a number of vendors rent canoes to paddle along the rivers and smaller creeks. Hikers can test the 21-mi Jackson

Red Ground Trail. You can also fish, but a state license is required. *11650 Munson Hwy., Milton 32570, tel. 850/957–6140, fax 850/957–6143, www.floridastateparks.org/blackwaterriver. $3.25 per car. Daily.*

CARVER-HILL MUSEUM ♦ Displayed here are memorabilia from Carver-Hill Elementary and High School, which operated 1954–69 as a blacks-only school. When integration shut the school's doors, students petitioned for keepsakes, including band and sports trophies, to be saved, and the museum was set up as a place to store them. Graduates update their personal histories inside. The museum is an official stop on the Florida Black Heritage Trail. *893 McClelland St., 32536, tel. 850/682–3494. Free. Weekdays 9–5; call for weekend hrs.*

ROBERT L. F. SIKES PUBLIC LIBRARY ♦ Named for the former resident and U.S. Senator, the town library is housed in an impressive Greek Revival building, which holds more than 44,000 volumes. *1445 Commerce Dr., 32539, tel. 850/682–4432. Free. Mon. and Tues. 10–8, Wed. and Thurs. 10–6, Fri. 8:30–4:30, Sat. 10–4.*

EAT

DESI'S ♦ Specializing in pastas, steaks, and salads, this casual restaurant has golf decorations on one side and animal prints on the other. The seafood fettucine has shrimp, scallops, and crab meat in a light Alfredo sauce with fettucine noodles, garlic bread, and a house salad. Friday is prime rib night. *$7–$13. 197 N. Main St., 32536, tel. 850/682–7477. MC, V. Closed weekends. No dinner Mon.–Wed.*

SONNY'S REAL PIT BBQ ♦ This primarily southern franchise restaurant is known for its grilled baby back ribs and sweet house barbecue sauce. The menu also includes barbecued hamburgers, sliced pork, sliced beef, and ribs. *$5–$11. 2680 S. Ferdon Blvd., 32536, tel. 850/683–0572. AE, D, MC, V.*

SLEEP

COMFORT INN ♦ This motel is off I–10, 5 mi from downtown Crestview. A marble, neo-Classical lobby has vases and columns, and the pastel exterior has fountains at the entryway. Rooms are standard motel-issue. *$80–$100. 4040 S. Ferdon Blvd., 32536, tel. 850/423–1200, fax 850/423–1210, www.comfortinn.com. 50 rooms. Complimentary Continental breakfast, in-room data ports, some in-room hot tubs, some kitchenettes, some microwaves, some refrigerators, cable TV, outdoor pool, no-smoking rooms. AE, D, DC, MC, V.*

CRESTVIEW HOLIDAY INN ♦ You'll find this simple stucco-and-sandstone motel at the intersection of Highway 85 and I–10. And you'll know you're in Florida when you see the shell-shape ceramic lamps, seashell-print bedspreads, and ocean-theme art on the walls. *$74. 4050 S. Ferdon Blvd., 32536, tel. 850/682–6111 or 800/465–4329, fax 850/689–1189, www.holiday-inn.com. 120 rooms. Restaurant, room service, in-room data ports, cable TV, outdoor pool, gym, bar, laundry facilities, some pets allowed (fee). AE, D, DC, MC, V.*

JAMESON INN ♦ This southeastern chain—which is found mostly in small towns—has hotels designed after elegant southern colonial mansions. Choose from one- and two-bedroom suites. From I–10, take Exit 12 and follow Highway 85 south to Cracker Barrel Drive. *$69–$89 room, $159 suite. 151 Cracker Barrel Dr., 32536, tel. 850/683–1778 or 800/526–3766, fax 850/683–1779, www.jamesoninns.com. 55 rooms; 2 suites. Complimentary Continental breakfast, in-room data ports, some kitchenettes, some microwaves, some refrigerators, cable TV, some in-room VCRs, outdoor pool, gym, laundry facilities, some pets allowed. AE, D, DC, MC, V.*

MORE INFO

CRESTVIEW AREA CHAMBER OF COMMERCE ♦ *502 S. Main St., Crestview 32536, tel. 850/682–3212, fax 850/683–7413, www. crestviewchamber.com.*

GETTING HERE

Crestview is directly off I–10 the junction of U.S. 90 and State Road 85. Fort Walton Beach, a military town and home to Eglin Air Force Base, lies 35 mi south of Crestview via State Road 85.

DE FUNIAK SPRINGS

Named for a prominent official of the Louisville and Nashville Railroad in the late 1800s, this Old Florida town of about 7,000 is midway between Alabama and the Gulf of Mexico in the panhandle. Walton County's seat is known for rich farmland and access to the white-sand beaches on the Gulf of Mexico, which are about 25 mi to the south. Thirty-five miles east of town, near Chipley, is Falling Waters State Recreation Area. The region's economy depends primarily on agriculture, but poultry and cattle are also raised and processed in the county.

SEE & DO

CHAUTAUQUA WINERY ♦ Opened in 1990, Chautauqua gives free tours of its facilities, where you can learn about the wine-making process and sample the vintages in the tasting room. The winery is off U.S. 331. *364 Hugh Adams Rd., 32433, tel. 850/892–5887, fax 850/892–8539. Free. Mon.–Sat. 9–5, Sun. noon–5.*

✪ **PONCE DE LEÓN SPRINGS STATE PARK** Some believe that Ponce de León Springs is the Spanish explorer's "fountain of youth." True or not, the sparkling 68°F water, which flows from a limestone cavity at the rate of 14 million gallons a day, is certainly refreshing. The spring flows into Sandy Creek and from there into the Choctawhatchee River, less than a mile to the south. A half-mile trail follows Sandy Creek, where you can picnic or fish. *2860 Ponce de León Springs Rd., Ponce de León 32455, tel. 850/836–4281 or 850/638–6130. $3.25 per vehicle. Daily 8 AM–dusk.*

WALTON-DE FUNIAK PUBLIC LIBRARY ♦ One of Florida's oldest libraries, this wood-frame building opened its doors in 1887. Today it contains nearly 30,000 volumes and a collection of antique weapons. *3 Circle Dr., tel. 850/892–3624, fax 850/892–4438. Free. Weekdays 9–5, Sat. 9–3.*

SLEEP

BEST WESTERN CROSSROADS INN ♦ Surrounded by 8 acres of pecan groves, this motel sits halfway between Tallahassee and Pensacola at the junction of I–10 and Highway 331. *$59–$79. 2343 Freeport Rd., 32433, tel. 850/892–5111, fax 850/892–2439, www. bestwestern.com. 100 rooms. Complimentary breakfast, restaurant, room service, cable TV, pool, bar, some pets allowed. AE, D, DC, MC, V.*

✪ **HOTEL DE FUNIAK** This tidy, old-fashioned hotel was built in 1920 and is now a B&B. Rooms are furnished with period antiques, some of which are original furnishings. It's one of the nicer places to stay in this part of the Panhandle. *$70 room; $120 suite. 400 E. Nelson Ave., 32433, tel. 850/892–4383 or 877/333–8642, fax 850/892–5346, www.hoteldefuniak.com. 8 rooms, 4 suites. Complimentary Continental breakfast, restaurant, cable TV, library; no smoking. AE, D, MC, V.*

MORE INFO

WALTON COUNTY CHAMBER OF COMMERCE ♦ *95 Circle Dr., De Funiak Springs 32435, tel. 850/892–3191, fax 850/892–9688, www. waltoncountychamber.com.*

GETTING HERE

De Funiak Springs is at the intersection of State Road 83 and U.S. 90, 28 mi east of Crestview. To get here from I–10, the main inland thoroughfare, exit at State Road 83 and proceed north 3 mi to the intersection of U.S. 90.

DESTIN

Fort Walton Beach's neighbor lies on the other side of the strait that connects Choctawhatchee Bay with the Gulf of Mexico. Destin takes its name from its founder, Leonard A. Destin, a Connecticut sea captain who settled his family here in the 1830s. For the next 100 years Destin remained a sleepy fishing village until the strait, or East Pass, was bridged in 1935. Then recreational anglers discovered its white sands, blue-green waters, and abundance of some of the most sought-after sport fish in the world. More billfish are hauled in around Destin each year than from all other Gulf fishing ports combined, giving credence to its nickname, the World's Luckiest Fishing Village. But you don't have to be the rod-and-reel type to love Destin. There's plenty to entertain the sand-pail set as well as senior citizens, and there are many nice restaurants, which you'll have an easier time finding if you remember that the main drag through town is referred to as both U.S. 98 and Emerald Coast Parkway. The name makes sense, but part of what makes the Gulf look so emerald in these parts is the contrasting whiteness of the sand on the beach. Actually, it's not sand—it's pure, powder-soft Appalachian quartz that was dropped off by a glacier a few thousand years back. Since quartz doesn't compress (and crews clean and rake the beach each evening), your tootsies get the sole-satisfying benefit of soft, sugary "sand."

SEE & DO

🦢 **BIG KAHUNA'S LOST PARADISE** ♦ In addition to a seasonal water park are year-round family attractions, including 54 holes of miniature golf, two go-kart tracks, an arcade, thrill rides for kids of all ages, and an amphitheater. *U.S. 98 E, tel. 850/837–4061, www.bigkahunas.com. Grounds free, water park $29.95, miniature golf $6.50, go-karts $6. Mid-Sept.–May, Fri. and Sat. 10 AM–midnight; June–mid-Sept., daily 10 AM–midnight. Water park closed mid-Sept.–Apr.*

EDEN STATE GARDENS ♦ Sixteen miles east of Destin, this was once the home of the Wesley Lumber Company's headquarters; it was one of many businesses involved in lumbering along the Gulf Coast between the 1890s and World War I. Today you can tour the Wesley family home and explore the 10½ acres of landscaped grounds, which are perfect for picnics. *181 Eden Garden Rd., Point Washington 32454, tel. 850/231–4214. $2 per vehicle, $1.50 for house tour. Grounds open daily; house tours Thurs.–Mon. 10–3.*

SHOP

The **Market at Sandestin** (9375 U.S. 98 W, tel. 850/267–8092) has 33 upscale shops that peddle such goods as expensive chocolates and designer clothes in an elegant minimall with boardwalks. It also has the area's only Starbucks Coffee franchise. ✪ **Silver Sands Factory Stores** (10562 Emerald Coast Pkwy., tel. 850/654–9771, www.silversandsoutlet.com) is one of the Southeast's largest retail outlets. More than 100 shops sell top-name merchandise that ranges from gifts to kids' clothes to menswear.

OUTDOORS

Pier-fish from the 3,000-foot-long Destin Catwalk, along the East Pass Bridge. **Adventure Charters** (East Pass Marina, 288 U.S. 98 E, tel. 850/654–4070, www.adventurecharters-destin.com) offers deep-sea, bay-bottom, and light-tackle fishing excursions. **East Pass Bait and Tackle** (East Pass Marina, 288 U.S. 98 E, tel. 850/837–2622) sells bait, tackle, and most anything else you'd need for a day of fishing.

The **Indian Bayou Golf & Country Club** (1 Country Club Dr., 32541, tel. 850/837–6192, www.indianbayougolf.com) has a 27-hole course. The 18-hole, Fred Couples–designed **Kelly Plantation Golf Club** (307 Kelly Plantation Dr., 32541, tel. 850/650–7600, www.kellyplantation.com) is a semiprivate course that runs along Choctawhatchee Bay. For sheer number of holes, the **Sandestin Golf and Beach Resort** (9300 Emerald Coast Pkwy. W, 32540, tel. 850/267–8211) tops the list, with 81.

Scuba-diving and snorkeling instruction and outings are available through **Emerald Coast Scuba** (110 Melvin St., tel. 850/837–0955 or 800/222–0955, www.divedestin.com).

The **Destin Racquet & Fitness Center** (995 Airport Rd., 32540, tel. 850/837–7300) has six Rubico courts. **Sandestin Golf and Beach Resort** (9300 Emerald Coast Pkwy. W, 32540, tel. 850/267–7110, www.sandestin.com/tennis), considered one of the nation's top tennis resorts, has 15 courts with grass, hard, and Rubico surfaces.

Harbor Walk Marina (66 U.S. 98 E, Destin 32541, tel. 850/337–8250) is a rustic-looking waterfront complex where you can get bait, gas, tackle, food, and anything else you might need for a day of fishing. Party fishing boat excursions cost as little as $55–$70, a cheaper alternative to chartering or renting your own boat.

Take diving lessons, arrange excursions, and rent all the necessary equipment at the **Scuba Shop** (348 Miracle Strip Pkwy., tel. 850/

243–1600). Don't expect clear Caribbean waters in the Gulf: visibility is about 20–50 feet, and diving depths range between 50 feet and 90 feet—not great, but not too bad.

AFTER DARK

Folks come by boat and car to **AJ's Club Bimini** (116 U.S. 98 E, tel. 850/837–1913, www.ajs/destin.com), a supercasual bar and restaurant overlooking a marina. Live music on weekends means young, lively crowds packing the dance floor. **Harbor Docks** (538 U.S. 98 E, tel. 850/837–2506) is another favorite with the local seafaring set. It's famous for live music and high-quality sushi. The **Hog's Breath Saloon** (541 E. U.S. 98 E, tel. 850/837–5991, www.hogsbreath.com), the original in a chain hot spot with other locations in Key West, Fort Walton Beach, and Cozumel, presents live music on weekends. The food—steaks, burgers, salads—isn't bad, either. Café Grazie's **Sky Bar** (1771 Old U.S. Hwy. 98 E, tel. 850/837–7475, www.skybar.com) draws a more mature crowd for dancing, cocktails, and live music.

EAT

AJ'S SEAFOOD ♦ This fun-filled family restaurant offers fantastic steamed or raw oysters as patrons dine to the laid-back tunes of Jimmy Buffett and others. *$9–$21. 116 U.S. 98 E, tel. 850/837–1913, www.ajs-destin.com. Reservations not accepted. AE, DC, MC, V.*

BACK PORCH ♦ Sea breezes will brush through your hair at this open wooden dining room overlooking the pristine white sand beaches and emerald green ocean. You can have just about any seafood dish prepared in the manner you desire: grilled, broiled, pan-fried, or steamed. The eatery is also known for its charcoal-grilled hamburgers. *$8–$20. 1740 Old U.S. Hwy. 98 E, 32540, tel. 850/837–2022. Reservations not accepted. AE, D, DC, MC, V.*

BISTRO BIJOUX ♦ Part of the Baytowne Wharf development at Sandestin Resort, this atmospheric spot serving Italian-tinged seafood became an instant local favorite when it opened in 2003. Starters include steamed mussels with garlic, fennel, and basil; cassoulet of shrimp and scallops; and fried-oyster salad with baby spinach and balsamic-bacon dressing. For dinner there's baked black grouper with artichokes and sun-dried tomatoes, seafood bouillabaisse, braised osso bucco, steaks, and pasta dishes. The bar, with its velvet occasional chairs, minimalist fireplace, and swank decor, is one of the classiest around. In fall or spring ask for a seat on the outdoor terrace overlooking the lagoon. *$21–$29. 9300 Emerald Coast Pkwy. W, tel. 850/622–0760. AE, D, DC, MC, V. No lunch.*

FLAMINGO CAFÉ ♦ Indoors, you'll find freshly starched white linen and refined elegance; outdoors, the patio is Florida casual all the way. Either way there's a panoramic view of Destin Harbor from every seat in the house, and boaters are welcome to tie up at the dock. The food is Floribbean—a mixture of Caribbean and Floridian elements. The chef is known for his special snapper and grouper dishes; try the delicious snapper en croûte—an oven-roasted snapper fillet layered in phyllo pastry with crabmeat and braised spinach in a cream sauce. *$19–$38. 414 U.S. 98 E, 32541, tel. 850/837–0961. AE, D, MC, V. No lunch.*

HARRY T'S BOAT HOUSE ♦ The dining rooms at this Destin Yacht Club restaurant overlook Destin Bay. The menu is mostly seafood, but there are also chicken and steak options. Try the grilled river grouper topped with crab and shrimp and served with a white wine and butter sauce, sprinkled with almonds. There are music and dancing here most nights. Tuesday is kids' night, when a clown entertains. This lively, fun restaurant was opened to honor the memory of trapeze artist "Flying Harry T." Babe. *$10–$22.*

320 U.S. Hwy. 98 E, 32541, tel. 850/654–4800, www.harryts.com. Reservations not accepted. AE, D, MC, V.

THE LIGHTHOUSE ♦ This family restaurant sits beneath a 60-foot mock lighthouse. The menu, of course, includes a wide variety of seafood, including salmon, mussels, and lobster, as well as local favorites such as prime rib. *$9–$27. 878 U.S. 98, tel. 850/654–2828. AE, D, DC, MC, V. No lunch weekends.*

LOUISIANA LAGNIAPPE ♦ In Louisiana when you say *lagniappe,* it means you're getting a little something extra—here it's the extra zing fresh local seafood gets when transformed into Cajun-style cuisine. You can't go wrong ordering Cajun standards like shrimp creole, crab bisque, and crawfish étouffée. Locals love the chef's innovations, such as grouper cocodrie, sautéed and topped with fried crawfish, artichoke hearts, and a rich béarnaise sauce. There's outside dining overlooking Destin Harbor, and you'll have delicious sunset views whether you're dining inside or out. *$15–$24. 775 Gulf Shore Dr., at Sandpiper Cove, tel. 850/837–0881. AE, D, DC, MC, V. No lunch.*

✪ MARINA CAFÉ A harbor view, impeccable service, and sophisticated fare create one of the finest dining experiences on the Emerald Coast. The ocean motif is expressed in shades of aqua, green, and sand accented with marine tapestries and sea sculptures. The chef calls his creations contemporary Continental, offering diners a choice of classic creole, Mediterranean, or PacificRim dishes. One regional specialty is the popular black pepper–crusted yellowfin tuna with braised spinach and spicy soy sauce. The menu changes daily, and the wine list is extensive. *$19–$35. 404 U.S. 98 E, 32541, tel. 850/837–7960, www.marinacafe. com. AE, D, DC, MC, V. No lunch.*

MCGUIRE'S IRISH PUB ♦ More than 225,000 single dollar bills, mementos from patrons, have been stuck to the bar and ceiling of this restaurant since it opened in 1977. USDA certified prime steaks and fresh seafood are the focus of the menu, though it also includes traditional Irish food, such as Irish lamb stew. Five house-made brews are on tap. The wine list includes over 350 bottles. There's entertainment nightly. *$10–$22. 33 U.S. 98 E, 32541, tel. 850/650–0000. AE, D, DC, MC, V.*

SLEEP

BEST WESTERN SUMMERPLACE INN ♦ In the heart of Destin, this four-story chain hotel with bay windows and arched galleries is convenient to the town's famous white sand beaches and emer-ald waters (about ¼ mi away), as well as area attractions and recre-ational activities. Some of the rooms have balconies and views of the Gulf. *$59–$179. 14047 Emerald Coast Pkwy. E, 32541, tel. 850/650–8003 or 888/232–2499, fax 850/650–8004, www.bestwestern.com. 72 rooms. Complimentary Continental breakfast, in-room data ports, some in-room hot tubs, some microwaves, refrigerators, cable TV, indoor-outdoor pool, outdoor hot tub, gym, sauna, laundry facilities, business services. AE, D, DC, MC, V.*

CLUB DESTIN RESORT ♦ This three-story, family-oriented resort is across Highway 98 from Destin Beach (about 1,000 feet.). A pri-vate access gate across the road leads to the beach. Even the small-est rooms have both a bed and sleeper sofa, so they can accommodate a small family. Check out the grand 70,000-gallon heated pool surrounded by a three-story tropical atrium. None of the rooms has a water view, but all have kitchen facilities. *$99 effi-ciency; $119 1-bedroom, $139 2-bedroom. 1085 U.S. 98, 32541, tel. 850/654–4700 or 888/983–3784, www.clubdestin.com. 120 rooms. Cable TV, indoor pool, gym, hot tub, putting green, children's programs (ages 4–12). AE, D, MC, V.*

HENDERSON PARK INN ♦ Tucked discreetly away at the end of a quiet road bordering Henderson Beach State Park, this B&B has become Destin's premier getaway for couples seeking elegance and pampering. A green mansard roof and shingle siding are reminiscent of Queen Anne–era architecture and complement the inn's Victorian-era furnishings. Each romantic room is furnished with a four-poster, canopied, or iron bed draped with fine linen. You'll find plush robes in all rooms, as well as balconies, perfect for admiring the Gulf's smashing sunsets. *$189–$334. 2700 Scenic U.S. 98 E, 32541, tel. 850/654–0400 or 800/336–4853, fax 850/654–0405, www.hendersonparkinn.com. 35 rooms. Restaurant, microwaves, refrigerators, cable TV, pool, beach; no kids (minimum age 25 or married). AE, D, MC, V.*

HIDDEN DUNES BEACH AND RESORT ♦ This 27-acre resort offers a range of accommodations, including cottages, condos, and villas, overlooking Destin's snowy white beaches. All units are equipped with kitchens and washers and dryers. The popular Carolina-style beach cottages are tucked away by spacious and private screened porches, shaded walkways, reflecting pools, and fountains. *$175–$395 7-night minimum summer, 3-night minimum winter. 9815 Hwy. 98 W, 32541, tel. 850/837–3521 or 800/824–6335, fax 850/654–9590, www.hiddendunes.com. 133 units. Restaurant, kitchenettes, microwaves, refrigerators, cable TV, 6 tennis courts, 3 pools, lake, hot tub, basketball, beach, laundry facilities. D, MC, V.*

✪ HILTON SANDESTIN This all-suites hotel is on the grounds of the lush Sandestin resort. Hilton guests can use Sandestin's beachfront golf courses as well as the Hilton's many other amenities, which include its own trio of heated pools. The majority of guest rooms have views of the water; all have balconies. *$229–$500 suites. 4000 Sandestin Blvd. S, 32550, tel. 850/267–9500 or 800/367–1271, fax 850/267–3076, www.sandestinbeachhilton. com. 598 suites. 2 restaurants, room service, in-room data ports, in-room safes, minibars, microwaves, refrigerators, cable TV, in-room VCRs with movies, driving range, 4 golf courses, putting green, 13 tennis courts, 3 pools, wading pool, gym, 2 hot tubs, massage, sauna, steam room, beach,* *bar, shops, children's programs (ages 5–12), business services. AE, D, DC, MC, V.*

HOLIDAY INN DESTIN ♦ Lounge on sugar-white sands, get to several golf courses with ease, and walk to some of Destin's amusement parks. Common areas jazzed up with skylights and greenery are spacious and eye-pleasing. The standard rooms are uniformly bright and well kept; prices vary depending on the view. *$165–$235. 1020 U.S. 98 E, 32541, tel. 850/837–6181, fax 850/837–1523, www.hidestin.com. 238 rooms. Restaurant, cable TV, 3 pools, beach, bar. AE, D, DC, MC, V.*

✪ SANDESTIN GOLF AND BEACH RESORT Newlyweds, conventioneers, and families all fit in at this 2,400-acre resort with villas, cottages, condominiums, boat slips, and an inn. Tennis buffs like it, too, because it's one of the few facilities on the Gulf Coast to offer grass, clay, and hardcourts. A recent addition is the Village of Baytowne Wharf, a "festival marketplace" of shops and restaurants; the Lagoons, a 7-acre family-friendly water park, is expected to open in 2008. All rooms have a view, either of the Gulf, Choctawhatchee Bay, a golf course, a lagoon, or a natural wildlife preserve. This resort accommodates an assortment of tastes, from the simple to the extravagant, but the gigantic suites at the Westwinds are a cut above the rest. *$89, $160–$215 suites, $215–$400 condos. 9300 Emerald Coast Pkwy. W, 32550, tel. 850/267–8000 or 800/277–0800, fax 850/267–8222, www.sandestin.com. 1200 accommodations (rooms, suites, and condos). 4 restaurants, cable TV, some kitchens, some microwaves, some refrigerators, cable TV, 4 18-hole golf courses, 16 tennis courts, pro shop, 11 pools, health club, beach, dock, 3 bars. AE, D, DC, MC, V.*

SEA OATS MOTEL ♦ Almost all rooms at this motel, 5 mi east of Destin, face the beach, which is right outside the door. Second-floor rooms have balconies. *$80–$158. 3420 Old Hwy. 98 E, 32541, tel. 850/837–6655 or 888/732–6287, fax 850/654–8255, www.seaoatsrentals.com. 42 rooms. Picnic area, some in-room hot tubs, some* *kitchenettes, some microwaves, some refrigerators, cable TV, pool, beach, laundry facilities, business services. D, MC, V.*

SEASCAPE RESORT AND CONFERENCE CENTER ♦ Across the road from the beach, this resort stands 6 mi east of Destin. The condos, all individually owned and appointed, do have balconies, though they do not have views of the Gulf. A small lake on the large property allows fishing (if you have a Florida license). *$95–$242 condominiums. 11625 U.S. Hwy. 98 E, 32550, tel. 850/837– 9181 or 800/874–9106, fax 850/837–4769, www.seascape-resort.com. 300 condominiums. Restaurant, some in-room hot tubs, kitchenettes, microwaves, refrigerators, cable TV, in-room VCRs, driving range, 18-hole golf course, putting green, tennis court, 5 pools, wading pool, basketball, fishing, bicycles, bar, business services. AE, D, DC, MC, V.*

SLEEP INN DESTIN ♦ One mile north of the beach and 8 mi east of Destin, this two-story motel sits across the highway from the Silver Sands Outlet Mall and its 100 stores. *$59–$125. 10775 W. Emerald Coast Pkwy., 32550, tel. 850/654–7022, fax 850/654–7022, www.choicehotels.com. 77 rooms. Complimentary Continental breakfast, some refrigerators, cable TV, pool, laundry facilities, business services. AE, D, DC, MC, V.*

TOPS'L BEACH MANOR ♦ Six miles east of Destin, this vast property, encircled by a nature preserve, occupies 53 acres on which there are three high-rise buildings (up to 15 stories tall). The resort is like a small town with shops, restaurants, and bars. Most condominiums have balconies overlooking the ocean. Ask about weekly rates if you're planning a longer stay. *$148–$236 1-bedroom condo; $136–$376 2-bedroom condo; $230–$437 villas; $326–$633 3-bedroom condo. 9011 Hwy. 98 W, 32550, tel. 850/267–9222 or 888/ 867–7535, www.abbottresorts.com. 300 units. Restaurant, kitchenettes, microwaves, refrigerators, cable TV, in-room VCRs with movies, putting green, 14 tennis courts, 4 pools (1 indoor), wading pool, gym, hot tub, sauna, steam room, racquetball, beach, business services. AE, D, MC, V.*

MORE INFO

DESTIN CHAMBER OF COMMERCE ♦ *4484 Legendary Dr., Destin 32541, tel. 850/837–6241, fax 850/654–5612, www.destinchamber. com.*

GETTING HERE

Destin is 8 mi east of Fort Walton beach on U.S. 98. To get here from I–10, the main inland artery, look for State Road 85 (Exit 56) and proceed south to State Road 20, then continue south to the Mid Bay Bridge. After crossing the bridge, continue south to U.S. 98 and turn right (heading east). Destin is 10 mi ahead.

FORT WALTON BEACH

This coastal town dates from the Civil War but had to wait more than 75 years to come into its own. Patriots loyal to the Confederate cause organized Walton's Guard (named in honor of Colonel George Walton, onetime acting Territorial governor of West Florida) and camped at a site on Santa Rosa Sound, later known as Camp Walton. In 1940 fewer than 90 people lived in Fort Walton Beach, but within a decade the city became a boomtown, thanks to New Deal money for roads and bridges and the development of Eglin Field during World War II. The military is now Fort Walton Beach's main source of income, but tourism runs a close second.

SEE & DO

AIR FORCE ARMAMENT MUSEUM ♦ Just outside the Eglin Air Force Base's main gate, this museum's collection contains more than 5,000 air force armaments from World Wars I and II and the Korean and Vietnam wars. Included are uniforms, engines, weapons, aircraft, and flight simulators; larger craft such as transport planes are exhibited on the grounds outside. A 32-minute movie about Eglin's history and its role in the development of armaments plays continuously. *Rte. 85, Eglin Air Force Base, tel. 850/ 882–4062, fax 850/882–3990. Free. Daily 9:30–4:30.*

EGLIN AIR FORCE BASE ♦ Encompassing 724 square mi of land, the base includes 10 auxiliary fields and 21 runways. Jimmie Doolittle's Tokyo Raiders trained here, as did the Son Tay Raiders, a group that made a daring attempt to rescue American POWs from a North Vietnamese prison camp in 1970. It's off-limits to civilians, but there are private tours for ROTC and military reunion groups. *Rte. 85, tel. 850/882–3931, www.eglin.af.mil.*

🐚 **GULFARIUM ♦** When the weather drives you off the beach, spend your time here. The main attraction is the Living Sea, a 60,000-gallon tank that simulates conditions on the ocean floor. See cheesy performances by trained porpoises, sea-lion shows, and marine-life exhibits. Don't overlook the old-fashioned Dolphin Reef gift shop, where you can buy anything from conch shells to beach toys. There's also a dolphin interaction program, but you don't swim with them. Instead, you sit in a pool as spotted dolphins swim up to your lap. *U.S. 98 E, tel. 850/243–9046 or 800/247–8575, www. gulfarium.com. $16, dolphin interaction $100. Daily 9–6.*

🐚 **INDIAN TEMPLE MOUND AND MUSEUM ♦** Kids especially enjoy this museum, where they can learn all about the prehistoric peoples who inhabited northwest Florida up to 10,000 years ago. It's a small museum, but the prehistoric Native American artifacts and weaponry on display are particularly fascinating, as are the few hands-on exhibits. The museum is adjacent to the 600-year-old **National Historic Landmark Temple Mound,** a large earthwork built near saltwater. *139 Miracle Strip Pkwy. (U.S. 98), tel. 850/833–9595. $2. Weekdays 10–4, Sat. 9–4.*

JOHN C. BEASLEY WAYSIDE PARK ♦ Fort Walton Beach's seaside playground is on Okaloosa Island. A boardwalk leads to the beach, where you'll find covered picnic tables, changing rooms, and freshwater showers. Lifeguards are on duty in summer. To get to Okaloosa Island from the mainland, just stay on U.S. Highway 98 (also known as State Road 30 as it passes through town). *Okaloosa Island, tel. 850/651–7131.*

PLEASURE ISLAND WATERPARK ♦ This water park has water-slides, wave runners, and volleyball and basketball in the activity pool. There's also a go-kart track. *1310 Hwy. 98 E, 32548, tel. 850/ 243–9738. $15. Mar.–Sept. daily 10–6.*

SHOP

Stores in the **Manufacturer's Outlet Center** (255 Miracle Strip Pkwy.) offer well-known brands of clothing and housewares at a substantial discount. There are four department stores in the **Santa Rosa Mall** (300 Mary Esther Cutoff, Mary Esther, tel. 850/ 244–2172), as well as 118 other shops, 15 bistro-style eateries, and a 10-screen movie theater.

OUTDOORS

Eglin Air Force Base Reservation is the size of Rhode Island— 724 square mi, 463,448 acres—and has 810 mi of creeks and plenty of challenging, twisting wooded trails. Biking at the reservation requires a $5 permit, which can be obtained from the Jackson Guard (107 Rte. 85 N, Niceville, tel. 850/882–4164).

The **Fort Walton Beach Golf Club** (Rte. 189, tel. 850/833–9529) is a 36-hole municipal course whose links (Oaks and Pines) lie about 1,000 yards from each other. The two courses are considered by many to be one of Florida's best public layouts. **Shalimar Pointe Golf & Country Club** (302 Country Club Dr., Shalimar, tel. 850/651–1416) has 18 holes with a pleasing mix of water and bunkers.

Play tennis on seven Rubico and two hard courts at the **Fort Walton Racquet Club** (1819 Hurlburt Rd., tel. 850/862–2023). The

Municipal Tennis Center (45 W. Audrey Dr., tel. 850/833–9588) has 12 lighted hard courts, four racquetball courts, and four practice walls.

AFTER DARK

Dueling pianos and a beachfront bar fuel the furious sing-alongs that make ✪ **Howl at the Moon** (1450 Miracle Strip Pkwy., tel. 850/301–0111, Closed Mon.), at the Boardwalk on Okaloosa Island, one of Fort Walton's most popular evening entertainment spots. The place rocks every night until 2 AM but can go as late as 4 AM in season.

Based in Fort Walton Beach, the **Northwest Florida Ballet** (tel. 850/664–7787) has presented classical and contemporary dance performances to audiences along the Gulf Coast for more than 30 years. Call for season schedule and ticket informationas well as their current performance venue.

EAT

CAFFÉ ITALIA ♦ This charming restaurant is known for its cappuccino and desserts. The *maremonti* (a penne pasta with shrimp and covered in a white sauce) is a local favorite. *$14–$24. 189 Brooks St., 32548, tel. 850/664–0035. AE, D, DC, MC, V. Closed Mon.*

KINFOLKS BAR-B-Q ♦ This casual eatery prides itself on open fire pit cooking. Of the four dishes served, the ribs and chicken is most popular. There's an additional kids' menu. *$5–$8. 333 Racetrack Rd. NW, 32547, tel. 850/863–5166. Reservations not accepted. No credit cards. Closed weekends.*

✪ **PANDORA'S STEAKHOUSE AND LOUNGE** On the Emerald Coast the name Pandora's is synonymous with prime rib. The weather-beaten exterior gives way to a warm and cozy interior with alcoves and tables for four. Steaks are cooked over a wood-burning grill, and you can order your prime rib regular or extra-cut; fish aficionados should try the char-grilled yellowfin tuna, bacon-wrapped and topped with Jamaican jerk sauce. The mood turns a bit more gregarious in the lounge, where there's live entertainment Wednesday through Saturday. *$13–$30. 1120 Santa Rosa Blvd., tel. 850/244–8669. AE, D, DC, MC, V. Closed Mon.*

STAFF'S ♦ Sip a Tropical Depression or a rum-laced Squall Line while you peruse a menu tucked into the centerfold of a tabloid-size newspaper filled with snippets of local history, early photographs, and family memorabilia. Since 1931 folks have been coming to this garage turned eatery for steaks and seafood dishes, such as freshly caught Florida lobster and char-grilled amberjack. The grand finale is a trip to the delectable dessert bar; try a generous wedge of cherry cheesecake. *$16–$29. 24 Miracle Strip Pkwy. SE, 32548, tel. 850/243–3482, fax 850/244–3326. AE, D, MC, V.*

SLEEP

DAYS INN ♦ This two-story motel is in the middle of Fort Walton Beach, 2 mi from the beach. There's a restaurant next door. *$68–$74. 135 Miracle Strip Pkwy., 32548, tel. 850/244–6184 or 800/544–8313, fax 850/244–5764, www.daysinn.com. 62 rooms. Complimentary Continental breakfast, in-room data ports, microwaves, refrigerators, cable TV, outdoor pool, some pets allowed. AE, D, DC, MC, V.*

LEESIDE INN & MARINA ♦ On this Okaloosa Island inn you can watch porpoises at play or take in the sunset from the dock. A 94-

slip marina is behind the complex, with a beach (and beachside bar) next door. Breakfast and dinner are served at the Jazz Café. *$75–$95. 1350 Miracle Strip Pkwy. SE, 32548, tel. 850/243–7359 or 800/824–2747, fax 850/243–2809, www.leesideinn.com. 104 rooms. Restaurant, some kitchenettes, some refrigerators, cable TV, outdoor pool, dock, boating, fishing, bar, laundry facilities, business services. AE, D, DC, MC, V.*

MARINA MOTEL ♦ This motel across the street from Choctawhatchee Bay offer many rooms with excellent ocean views. Restaurants are within walking distance. *$90–$120; $125 and up, suites. 1345 Miracle Strip Pkwy., 32548, tel. 800/237–7021 reservations or 850/244–1129, fax 850/243–6063. 36 rooms; 2 suites. Complimentary Continental breakfast, some kitchenettes, microwaves, refrigerators, cable TV, outdoor pool, docks, boating, fishing, laundry facilities, some pets allowed (fee). AE, D, DC, MC, V.*

✪ RADISSON BEACH RESORT This U-shape hotel consists of a six-story tower flanked by three-story wings. Rooms have pastel green-and-peach color schemes and face either the Gulf or one of the pools, although even poolside rooms have a bit of a sea view. *$79–$189. 1110 Santa Rosa Blvd., 32548, tel. 850/243–9181, fax 850/664–7652, www.radisson.com. 287 rooms. Restaurant, in-room date ports, cable TV, 2 tennis courts, 3 pools, gym, beach, bar, Internet. AE, D, DC, MC, V.*

RAMADA PLAZA BEACH RESORT ♦ Activity here revolves around a heated pool with a grotto and swim-through waterfall; there's also an 800-foot private beach. All rooms have refrigerators, but the twin double beds are the only sleeping option. *$140–195, $250–$280 suites. 1500 Miracle Strip Pkwy. SE, 32548, tel. 800/874–8962 or 850/243–9161, fax 850/243–2391, www. ramadafwb.com. 309 rooms; 26 suites. 2 restaurants, refrigerators, cable TV with movies and video games, 2 pools, gym, beach, 3 bars, Internet. AE, D, DC, MC, V.*

MORE INFO

GREATER FORT WALTON CHAMBER OF COMMERCE ♦ *34 Miracle Strip Pkwy. SE, Box 640, Fort Walton 32549, tel. 850/244–8191, fax 850/244–1935, www.destin-fwb.com.*

GETTING HERE

Fort Walton Beach is on U.S. 98, 35 mi west of Pensacola Beach on the Gulf of Mexico. From I–10, take State Road 85 south 35 mi.

GRAYTON BEACH

The 26-mi stretch of coastline between Destin and Panama City Beach is referred to as the Beaches of South Walton. Add to the sun and fun at these amazing beaches enough good restaurants to make selecting a dinner spot the day's most challenging decision. Accommodations consist primarily of private-home rentals, the majority of which are managed by local real estate firms. Also scattered along Route 30 A are a few small boutiques, with hand-painted furniture, jewelry, and contemporary gifts and clothing. Inland, thick pine forests and hardwoods surround the area's 14 lakes, giving anglers ample spots to drop a line. Grayton Beach, the oldest community in this area, has reached its 100-year mark. You can still see some of the old weathered cypress homes scattered along sandy streets. The town has made some minor concessions to growth in the way of a small market and a couple of restaurants in its single-road "downtown" district. Don't expect much more. Stringent building restrictions, designed to protect the pristine beaches, ensure that Grayton maintains its small-town feel and look.

SEE & DO

EDEN STATE GARDENS ♦ An antebellum mansion called the Wellesley House is ensconced among moss-cloaked live oaks and gardens. Don't miss it if you're here in mid-March, when the dogwoods and azaleas are in full bloom. *Rte. 395, Point Washington 32458, tel. 850/231–4214. $2. Daily 8 AM–dusk; tours of Wellesley House Thurs.–Mon. 10–3.*

✪ GRAYTON BEACH STATE PARK The 2,133-acre park is one of the most scenic spots along the Gulf Coast. Composed primarily of untouched Florida woodlands, it also has salt marshes, rolling dunes covered with sea oats, crystal-white sand, and contrasting blue-green waters. The park offers facilities for swimming, fishing, snorkeling, and camping. Even if you're just passing by, the beach here is worth the stop. Thirty new cabins are now available for rent. *357 Main Park Rd., tel. 850/231–4210. $3.25 per vehicle, up to 8 people. Daily 8 AM–dusk.*

SHOP

Gaffrey Art Gallery (21 Blue Gulf Dr., 3 mi west of Grayton Beach, Santa Rosa Beach, tel. 850/267–0228) sells hand-painted furniture and furniture handmade by the Gaffrey family. Under the shade trees of Grayton Beach, **Magnolia House** (2 Magnolia St., 32459, tel. 850/231–5859, www.magnoliahouse.com) sells gift items, bath products, and accessories for the home. The **Shops of Grayton** (Rte. 283 [Grayton Rd.], 2 mi south of U.S. 98, no phone) is a colorful complex of eight Cracker-style cottages where you'll find gifts, artwork, and antiques. **Wild Women Art Gallery** (39 Blue Gulf Dr., Blue Mt. Beach, tel. 850/653–4099, fax 850/653–4154), which sells "art for the wild at heart," carries adorable hand-painted children's furniture, prints, artwork, and glass.

OUTDOORS

The **Santa Rosa Golf & Beach Club** (Rte. 30 A, Santa Rosa Beach, tel. 850/267–2229) is a semiprivate 18-hole course that, thankfully, has little residential development beside the fairways.

AFTER DARK

The **Red Bar** (70 Hotz Ave., tel. 850/231–1008), the local watering hole, is elbow to elbow on Friday and Saturday nights, when red-hot bands play blues and jazz.

EAT

✪ **CRIOLLAS** Inventive, contemporary, and constantly changing fare continues to win local raves for this spot. You might choose to experience Island Hopping—a three-course dinner focusing on a particular Caribbean region. The region varies from month to month, so returning diners can sample a different cuisine each visit. *$19–$35. 170 E. Hwy. 30 A, tel. 850/267–1267, fax 850/231–4568. AE, D, MC, V. Closed Sun. and Mon. Nov.–Jan. No lunch.*

PANDORA'S ◆ The thatched bamboo ceiling and outdoor tiki bar and deck with live music on weekends give this casual family restaurant a real beach vibe (though it's a few blocks away from the water). Popular dishes include lobster snow crab, grouper, and six different cuts of steak. *$15–$32. 63 DeFuniak St., 32459, tel. 850/231–4102. AE, D, DC, MC, V. Closed Sun.–Tues.*

✪ **PICOLO RESTAURANT & RED BAR** You could spend weeks here just taking in all the eclectic memorabilia—from Marilyn Monroe posters to flags to dolls—dangling from the ceiling and tacked to every available square inch of wall. The equally contemporary menu is small, changes daily, and is very Floridian. A baked-eggplant dish stuffed with shrimp, scallops, and grilled vegetables is a popular entrée. Live blues and jazz play nightly in season. *$10–$18. 70 Hotz Ave., 32459, tel. 850/231–1008, fax 850/231–4191. No credit cards.*

SLEEP

CABINS AT GRAYTON BEACH STATE PARK ♦ Back-to-nature enthusiasts and families like these basic yet stylish accommodations among the sand pines and scrub oaks of this pristine state park. The two-bedroom, tin-roof accommodations, which have white trim and tropical wooden window louvers, come with air-conditioning and full-size kitchens complete with pots and pans. There's no daily maid service—fresh linens are provided, however—and no room phones, but gas fireplaces, barbecue grills, and screen porches add a homey touch. *$85–$110. 357 Main Park Rd., Santa Rosa Beach 32459, tel. 800/326–3521 for reservations, www.reserveamerica.com. 30 cabins. Kitchens; no room phones, no room TVs. AE, MC, V.*

HIBISCUS COFFEE & GUESTHOUSE ♦ Ten minutes from the beach is this quaint, two-story complex with gardens. The simple and very clean rooms are tastefully adorned with small artistic prints. The Art Deco Room and Hibiscus Rooms have claw-foot tubs. A café downstairs serves breakfast and lunch. *$85–$140. 85 DeFuniak St., 32459, tel. 850/231–2733, fax 850/231–4158, www.hibiscusflorida.com. 4 rooms. Restaurant, cable TV, bicycles, library, laundry facilities. MC, V.*

MORE INFO

SOUTH WALTON TOURIST DEVELOPMENT COUNCIL ♦ *25777 U.S. Hwy. 331 S, Santa Rosa Beach 32459, tel. 850/267–1216 or 800/ 822–6877, fax 850/267–3943, www.beachesofsouthwalton.com.*

GETTING HERE

Grayton Beach is 18 mi east of Destin, or 5 mi west of Seaside, on Route 30 A. From I–10, take U.S. 331 south to Highway 98 east and follow the signs. Many of the roads in the little town are unpaved and can get bumpy after rain or dusty in dry spells. Few of the roads are clearly marked, so locals tend to give directions using structures as landmarks, not by using the official names of roads.

GULF BREEZE

This pretty Florida Panhandle resort town of 5,000, at the tip of the peninsula that separates Pensacola Bay from its barrier islands, has miles of beaches on the Gulf of Mexico. The town can trace its history back to 1936, when the Gulf Breeze Cottages and store opened on the narrow peninsula. Today its economy relies on the presence of the U.S. Navy and a vast range of recreational activities, including fishing, sailing, swimming, and diving, which draw tourists in large numbers.

SEE & DO

✪ **THE ZOO** Catch a ride on the Safari Line train for an up-close excursion through 30 acres of roaming animals in their natural habitat. You can see everything from orangutans to bears to alligators. *5701 Gulf Breeze Pkwy., Gulf Breeze 32563, tel. 850/932–2229, fax 850/932–8575. $10.95. Daily 9–5.*

SHOP

Harbourtown Shopping Village (913 Gulf Breeze Pkwy.) has trendy shops and the look of a wharfside New England village.

OUTDOORS

Tiger Point Golf & Country Club (1255 Country Club Rd., tel. 850/932–1330, fax 850/934–3701, www.tigerpointclub.com) is a semiprivate 36-hole club.

EAT

CANCUN MEXICAN GRILL ◆ Note the large and realistic ocean-front mural as you enter this eatery known for chicken fajitas and quesadillas. There's outdoor dining on a patio and a kids' menu. *$5–$11. 1385 Shoreline Dr., 32561, tel. 850/916–4520. AE, D, MC, V.*

SLEEP

BAY BEACH INN ◆ This hotel comprises three two-story buildings on Pensacola Bay. It's 6 mi from Pensacola Beach and 5 mi from the zoo. *$69–$89, $99 suites. 51 Gulf Breeze Pkwy., 32561, tel. 850/ 932–2214, fax 850/932–0932, www.baybeachinn.com. 160 rooms; 8 suites in 3 buildings. Restaurant, in-room data ports, some microwaves, some refrigerators, cable TV, pool, wading pool, laundry service, business services, some pets allowed (fee). AE, D, DC, MC, V.*

MORE INFO

GULF BREEZE AREA CHAMBER OF COMMERCE ◆ *409 Gulf Breeze Pkwy., Gulf Breeze 32561, tel. 850/932–7888, fax 850/934–4601, www.gulfbreezechamber.com.*

GETTING HERE

The town of Gulf Breeze sits on a barrier island between Pensacola and Pensacola Beach. To get here from Pensacola, take U.S. 98 east out of town across the Pensacola Bay Bridge; Gulf Breeze is on the east side of the bridge. To get here from Pensacola Beach (Santa Rosa Island), take the coastal highway (State Road 399) west toward Pensacola, crossing the Bob Sikes Bridge; Gulf Breeze is on the west side of the bridge. From Destin, simply head west on U.S. 98 for 35 mi.

MARIANNA

Fifteen miles south of the Alabama border, this 10-square-mi town on the banks of the Chipola River is called home by about 6,200 residents. Marianna has been called one of the top 100 best small towns in America, the only Florida town to earn the distinction. With its proximity to Florida Caverns State Park, it's a good place to have lunch or grab a picnic before heading into the caves.

SEE & DO

CHIPOLA RIVER ♦ Locals favor this north–south river for swimming, canoeing, rafting, and kayaking. You get to the river at Spring Creek Park along Highway 90 E.

✪ FLORIDA CAVERNS STATE PARK Take a ranger-led cave tour to see stalactites, stalagmites, and "waterfalls" of solid rock at this expansive park. Some of the caverns are off-limits to the public or open for scientific study only with a permit, but you'll still see enough to fill a half day or more. Between Memorial Day and Labor Day, rangers offer guided lantern tours on Friday and Saturday nights. There are also hiking trails, campsites, and areas for swimming and canoeing on the Chipola River. *3345 Caverns Rd., tel. 850/482–9598, 850/482–1228 camping reservations, fax 850/ 482–9114, www.floridastateparks.org/floridacaverns. Park $3.25 per vehicle, up to 8 people; caverns $5. Daily 8 AM–dusk, cavern tours daily 9–4:30.*

THREE RIVERS STATE PARK ♦ The Chattahoochee and Flint rivers merge, becoming the Apalachicola River. You can wildlife-watch on the 2-mi nature trails of this 680-acre park; alligators and snapping turtles are commonly seen around Lake Seminole. Fishing, birding, and camping are popular in the 30-site camp-ground. *7908 Three Rivers Park Rd., Exit 23 off Rte. 10; 25 mi east on U.S. 90, then 2 mi north on Hwy. 271, tel. 850/482–9006, www. floridastateparks.org/threeriver, fax 850/593–6505. Day visitors, $3.25 per vehicle; campers $8–$12. Daily 8 AM–dusk.*

EAT

✪ RED CANYON GRILL Native American items and other south-western artifacts furnish the interior at this restaurant, 2 mi north of Marianna. The antler chandelier adds a further rustic touch. Most dishes are cooked on an open flame on the pecan wood–fired grill. Try the pecan-and-sage crusted chicken breast, or wood-grilled rib-eye steak, along with wood-grilled vegetables and pasta. You can eat in the main dining room or the cantina, off to the side. *$9–$15. 3297 Caverns Rd., tel. 850/482–4256. AE, MC, V. Closed Sun. and Mon. No lunch.*

TONY'S ♦ With booths and checkered tablecloths, this place is in-expensive and fun for families and a hangout for locals. They serve a mix of traditional Italian dishes and local fare, such as fried cat-fish with hush puppies and a side of candied yams. *$7–$16. 4133 W. Lafayette St., tel. 850/482–2232. AE, D, MC, V. Closed Sun.*

SLEEP

COMFORT INN ◆ Just off I–10, this two-story motor inn is 4 mi south of Marianna. It's close to several restaurants and to Florida Caverns State Park. *$55–$80. 2175 Hwy. 71, Exit 21 off I–10, 32446, tel. 850/526–5600, fax 850/482–7899, www.comfortinn.com. 80 rooms. Complimentary Continental breakfast, in room data ports, cable TV, pool, laundry service, business services, some pets allowed. AE, D, DC, MC, V.*

✪ **HINSON HOUSE B&B** Built in 1920, the house stands at the center of town where the Civil War Battle of Marianna was fought. Rooms and common areas both are furnished in period antiques. Wine and beverages are offered each evening. *$55–$85. 4338 Lafayette St., 32446, tel. 850/526–1500, 800/531–4786 (plus PIN, or extension, 1500), www.phonl.com/hinson_house. 5 rooms. Complimentary breakfast, cable TV; no smoking. AE, D, MC, V.*

MORE INFO

JACKSON COUNTY CHAMBER OF COMMERCE ◆ *4318 Lafayette St., Box 130, Marianna 32446, tel. 850/482–8061, fax 850/482–8002, www.jcflchamber.com.*

GETTING HERE

To get to Marianna from I–10, the Panhandle's main inland thoroughfare, exit at U.S. 231 and head north 2 mi. Marianna is at the intersection of U.S. 231 and U.S. 90.

NICEVILLE

Niceville lives up to its name. It's close to Destin and Fort Walton Beach, and 12 mi north of the Gulf of Mexico. Both Niceville and its twin city, Valparaiso, were first settled at the beginning of the 20th century and were granted their charters in 1938 and 1921, respectively. Today, their combined populations are over 36,000. The surrounding forests provided a rich source for the logging industry, as well as the turpentine stills that flourished in the early 1900s. The other major industry was fishing, in the inland waterways around Choctawhatchee Bay. Now the largest employer is Eglin Air Force Base.

SEE & DO

FRED GANNON ROCKY BAYOU STATE RECREATIONAL AREA ♦
This 357-acre park, 5 mi east of Niceville, is relatively undiscovered, so you can find some peace and quiet not far from civilization. You can hike, picnic, and boat, or even camp overnight at one of the 42 campsites (water and electric hook-ups). Mountain bikers are welcome to try some of the difficult trails. Campground reservations can be made up to 11 months in advance. *4281 State Road 20 E, 32578, tel. 850/833–9144, www.*

floridastateparks.org/rockybayou. $2 per vehicle; camping $8–$10 per night. Daily 8 AM–dusk.

TURKEY CREEK WALK ♦ Travel this 5-mi boardwalk over the creek and through 20 acres of countryside to view wildlife and indigenous landscapes. *John Sims Pkwy., tel. 850/729–4062.*

OUTDOORS

Bluewater Bay Resort (2000 Bluewater Bay Blvd., Niceville, tel. 850/897–3241 or 800/874–2128), 6 mi east of Niceville via Route 20 east, has 36 holes of championship golf on courses designed by Jerry Pate and Tom Fazio.

SLEEP

BLUEWATER BAY GOLF & TENNIS RESORT ♦ Popular for its 36 holes of championship golf (on courses designed by Jerry Pate and Tom Fazio), this upscale resort is 12 mi north of Destin via the Mid-Bay Bridge on the shores of Choctawhatchee Bay. It has all sorts of vacation rentals, from motel rooms to villas to patio homes. *$80–$220. 1940 Bluewater Blvd., Niceville 32578, tel. 850/897–3613 or 800/874–2128, fax 850/897–2424, www.bwbresort.com. 85 units. Restaurant, cable TV, 36-hole golf course, 19 tennis courts, 4 pools, bar, playground. AE, D, DC, MC, V.*

MORE INFO

NICEVILLE-VALPARAISO BAY AREA CHAMBER OF COMMERCE ♦ *1055 E. John Sims Pkwy., Valparaiso 32578, tel. 850/678–2323, fax 850/678–2602, www.nicevillechamber.com.*

GETTING HERE

To get to Niceville from I–10, the main inland thoroughfare, take State Road 85 south 15 mi to the Niceville–Valparaiso area. To get here from the coast, take U.S. 98 to State Road 293 north, which crosses Choctawhatcheee Bay on the Mid-Bay Bridge and then connects with State Road 85; follow it north 7 mi to Niceville.

PANAMA CITY BEACH

Despite the shoulder-to-shoulder condominiums, motels, and amusement parks that make it seem like one big carnival ground, this coastal resort has a natural beauty that, in some areas, such as St. Andrew's State Park, manages to excuse its gross overcommercialization. Public beaches along the Miracle Strip combine with video-game arcades, miniature golf courses, sidewalk cafés, souvenir shops, and shopping centers to lure people. The incredible white sands, navigable waterways, and plentiful marine life that attracted Spanish conquistadors bring family vacationers today. Summer holiday weekends are especially busy with regional visitors from Alabama and Georgia, but Spring Break is best avoided altogether—unless you want to rub elbows with tens of thousands of party-crazed college kids.

SEE & DO

BAY POINT'S LAGOON LEGEND AND MEADOWS GOLF COURSES ♦ Play 36 holes on these challenging courses at Marriott's Bay Point resort, with the eponymous lagoon waiting at the 16th hole of the Lagoon Legend course. These par-72 courses have some of the highest slope ratings in the country and are consistently ranked among the best in the state. Tee times can be booked two months in advance. *4701 Bay Point Rd., 32411, tel. 850/ 235–6937. $70 morning, $60 after 11 AM, $42.50 after 1 PM. Daily dawn–dusk.*

COUNTY PIER ♦ You can catch anything from shark to flounder from this 1,000-foot wooden fishing pier. Rod and reel rentals are available, and the adjacent beach offers sailing, windsurfing, kayaking, swimming, and a marine mammal attraction. *12213 Front Beach Rd., 32417, tel. 850/236–1009. Free. Daily.*

☾ **GULF WORLD** ♦ The resident marine park, which covers 6½ acres, has a tropical garden, tropical bird theater, and alligator and otter exhibits. The shark-feeding and scuba demonstrations are popular with the kids, but the old favorites—performing sea lions, otters, and bottle-nosed dolphins—still hold their own. *15412 Front Beach Rd., tel. 850/234–5271, fax 850/235–8957, www. gulfworldmarinepark.com. $19.42. Late May–early Sept., daily 9–4; call for hrs at other times of year.*

☾ **MIRACLE STRIP AMUSEMENT PARK** ♦ Enjoy dozens of rides here from a traditional Ferris wheel to a roller coaster with a 65-foot drop. *12000 Front Beach Rd., tel. 850/234–5810, www. miraclestrippark.com. $17. Apr. and May, Fri. and Sat. 6 PM–11 PM; June–early Sept., Sun.–Fri. 6 PM–11 PM, Sat. 2 PM–11:15 PM.*

☾ **MUSEUM OF MAN IN THE SEA** ♦ See rare examples of breathing apparatus and diving equipment, some dating as far back as the 1600s, in addition to exhibits on Florida's historic shipwrecks. There are also treasures recovered from famous wrecks, including artifacts from the Spanish galleon *Atocha,* and live creatures found in the area's coastal waters. *17314 Panama City Beach Pkwy., 32413, tel. 850/235–4101, www.diveweb.com/iod/mmits.html. $5. Daily 9–5.*

☾ **SHIPWRECK ISLAND** ♦ The Miracle Strip Amusement Park also operates Shipwreck Island, a 6-acre water park offering everything from speedy slides and tubes to the slow-moving Lazy River.

12000 Front Beach Rd., tel. 850/234–0368, www.shipwreckisland.com. $22.50. Mid-Apr.–May, weekends 10:30–5; June–early Sept., daily 10:30–5.

✪ ☙ **ST. ANDREWS STATE PARK** At the eastern tip of Panama City Beach, the park includes 1,260 acres of beaches, pinewoods, and marshes. There are complete camping facilities here, as well as places to swim, pier-fish, or hike the dunes along clearly marked nature trails. Board a ferry to **Shell Island**—a barrier island in the Gulf of Mexico with some of the best shelling north of Sanibel Island. An artificial reef creates a calm, shallow play area that is perfect for young children. Come to this spectacular park for a peek at what the entire beach area looked like before developers got ahold of it. *4607 State Park La., tel. 850/233–5140. $4 per vehicle, up to 8 people. Daily 8 am–dusk.*

ZOO WORLD ♦ This 7½-acre zoological preserve and botanical garden is known for allowing you to get close to the animals. You can, for example, feed the giraffes and llamas. *9008 Front Beach Rd. 32407, tel. 850/230–1065, fax 850/230–8500. $11.95. Daily 9–4:30.*

SHOP

Stores in the **Manufacturer's Outlet Center** (105 W. 23rd St., Panama City) offer well-known brands at a substantial discount. The **Panama City Mall** (2150 Martin Luther King Jr. Blvd., Panama City 32405, tel. 850/785–9587) has a mix of more than 100 franchise shops and national chain stores.

OUTDOORS

Rentals for a trip down Econofina Creek, "Florida's most beautiful canoe trail," are supplied by **Econofina Creek Canoe**

Livery (Strickland Rd., north of Rte. 20, Youngstown 32466, tel. 850/722–9032).

Find pari-mutuel betting (a type of cooperative wagering) year-round and live greyhound racing five nights and two afternoons a week at the **Ebro Greyhound Park.** Simulcasts of Thoroughbred racing from the Miami area are also shown throughout the year. Schedules change periodically, so call for details. *6558 Dog Track Rd., Ebro 32437, tel. 850/234–3943, www.ebrogreyhoundpark.com. General $2, clubhouse $1 extra.*

The **Hombre Golf Club** (120 Coyote Pass, tel. 850/234–3673, www.hombregolfclub.com) has a 27-hole course that occasionally hosts professional tours. **Marriott's Bay Point Resort** (4200 Marriott Dr., 32408, tel. 850/236–6000 or 800/874–7105, www.marriottbaypoint.com) has a country club that has 36 holes open to the public.

✪ **Shell Island Trips.** Narrated three-hour boat tours, from Captain Anderson's Marina at Grand Lagoon, take you to uninhabited Shell Island. Along the way, you can look for dolphins; on the way back, the boat cruises around St. Andrew's Bay. *5550 N. Lagoon, 32408, tel. 850/234–3435. $16. Mar.–Oct., daily 1–4.*

AFTER DARK

Club La Vela (8813 Thomas Dr., tel. 850/235–1061, www.clublavela.com) might also be known as the club that MTV built. The spring-break crowd has 48 bar stations, 14 dance floors, and three band stages to choose from in season, but there's something going on year-round. Broadway touring shows, top-name entertainers, and concert artists are booked into the **Marina Civic Center** (8 Harrison Ave., Panama City 32408, tel. 850/769–1217 or 850/763–4696). **Pineapple Willy's** ($6–$19, 9875 S. Thomas Dr., tel. 850/235–0928, www.pineapplewillys.com) is an eatery and bar geared toward families and tourists—as well as sports fans. **Schooner's** (5121 Gulf Dr., tel. 850/235–3555, www.schooners.com), a beachfront bar and restaurant, draws huge crowds of mostly locals for live music and late-night dancing on weekends.

EAT

ANGELO'S STEAK PIT ♦ This western-style restaurant has been around since 1957. The 8- to 32-ounce USDA choice corn-fed steer steaks are cooked on an open-pit hickory fire. There are N.Y. strip sirloin, baby back ribs, filet mignon, and rib eye, among other choice cuts. *$13–$23. 9527 Front Beach Rd. (Hwy. 98), 32407, tel. 850/234–2531, www.angelos-steakpit.com. Reservations not accepted. AE, D, MC, V. Closed early Oct.–mid-Mar. Closed Sun. mid-Mar.–Memorial Day. No lunch.*

BILLY'S STEAMED SEAFOOD RESTAURANT, OYSTER BAR, AND CRAB HOUSE ♦ Roll up your sleeves and dig into some of the Gulf's finest blue crabs and shrimp seasoned to perfection with Billy's special recipe. Homemade gumbo, crawfish, and the day's catch, plus sandwiches and burgers, round out the menu. The taste here is in the food, not the surroundings, but you can eat on an outdoor patio in the cooler months—if you don't mind the hum of traffic on busy Thomas Drive. *$5–$20. 3000 Thomas Dr., 32408, tel. 850/235–2349. AE, D, MC, V.*

BOAR'S HEAD ♦ An exterior that looks like an oversize thatch-roof cottage sets the mood for dining in this ersatz-rustic restaurant and tavern. Prime rib has been the number one people-pleaser since the house opened in 1978, but blackened seafood and broiled shrimp with crabmeat stuffing are popular, too. *$14–$30. 17290 Front Beach Rd., tel. 850/234–6628, www.boarsheadrestaurant.com. AE, D, DC, MC, V. No lunch.*

CAPT. ANDERSON'S ♦ Come early to watch the boats unload the catch of the day on the docks, and be among the first to line up to eat in this noted restaurant. A nautical theme is reinforced by tables made of hatch covers, and in the attached bar, which attracts long-time locals, the old-school interior is frozen in a 1960s time warp, but charmingly so. The Greek specialties aren't limited to feta cheese and shriveled olives; charcoal-broiled fish and steaks have a prominent place on the menu. If you're visiting in the off-season, call to make sure they are adhering to the posted hours before venturing out. *$12–$38. 5551 N. Lagoon Dr., tel. 850/234– 2225. Reservations not accepted. AE, D, DC, MC, V. Closed Nov.–Feb. and Sun. No lunch.*

HAMILTON'S ♦ Waterfront dining takes place in a gorgeous Victorian-style complex overlooking Grand Lagoon, with antiques, stained glass, and hardwood floors. The 5,000-square-foot second level deck is a great place to watch the sunset. Specialties include shrimp scampi, blackened tuna, shellfish with angel hair pasta, chicken teriyaki, and BBQ chicken. A mesquite grill cooks steaks and certain seafood dishes. *$15–$26. 5711 N. Lagoon Dr., 32408, tel. 850/234–1255, www.hamiltonspcbeach.com. Reservations not accepted. AE, D, MC, V. No lunch.*

✪ SCHOONER'S Billing itself as the "last local beach club," this beachfront spot is the perfect place for a casual family lunch or early dinner: kids can have burgers and play on the beach while you enjoy grown-up drinks and homemade gumbo, steak, or simply prepared seafood. Late-night crowds pile in for live music and dancing. *$6–$24. 5121 Gulf Dr., tel. 850/235–3555, www.schooners. com. AE, D, MC, V.*

SLEEP

BOARDWALK BEACH RESORT ♦ Two family-oriented hotels—the Howard Johnson and Convention Center Hotel—cling to this mile of beach front despite the incursion of timeshares (two other hotels in the resort were razed to make room for condos). Although this resort is not as glitzy as some of its neighbors, its clean appearance and reasonable prices are hard to beat. All share the long beach, and group parties are given regularly. Each has its own pool. *$59–$179. 9450 S. Thomas Dr., 32408, tel. 850/234–3484 or 800/224–4853, fax 850/233–4369, www.boardwalkbeachresort.com. 300 units. 2 restaurants, some microwaves, some refrigerators, cable TV, 3 pools, beach, video game room, playground. AE, D, DC, MC, V.*

DOLPHIN INN MOTEL AT PINEAPPLE BEACH ♦ Part of Pineapple Resorts, along with its sister property Pineapple Villas, the three-story inn is right on the beach with a seasonal tiki bar, sun deck, and barbecue and picnic areas beside the beachfront pool. All rooms have ocean views. *$70–$125. 19935 Front Beach Rd. (Hwy. 98), 32413, tel. 850/234–1788 or 800/234–1788, www.pineapplebeachresort.com. 30 rooms. Kitchenettes, in-room data ports, microwaves, refrigerators, cable TV, some in-room VCRs, pool, beach, laundry facilities, free parking, some pets allowed (fee). AE, D, MC, V.*

✪ **EDGEWATER BEACH RESORT** Luxurious one-, two-, and three-bedroom apartments in beachside towers and golf-course villas are elegantly furnished with wicker and rattan. The resort centerpiece is a Polynesian-style lagoon pool with waterfalls, reflecting ponds, footbridges, and more than 20,000 species of tropical plants. This resort is a good option for longer stays or family vacations. *$100–$300. 11212 Front Beach Rd., 32407, tel. 850/235–4044 or 800/ 874–8686, fax 850/233–7529, www.edgewaterbeachresort.com. 520 apartments. 3 restaurants, cable TV, 9-hole golf course, 11 pools, 11 tennis courts, hair salon, spa, beach, 2 bars, recreation room. D, DC, MC, V.*

HOLIDAY INN SUNSPREE RESORT ♦ All rooms have private balconies with ocean views at this 14-story resort. The curving building embraces the white sands of the beach and a huge heated pool with waterfalls, lush tropical planting, and many palm trees. A wide range of activities includes karaoke, live entertainment, and a Polynesian torch lighting ceremony every night at sunset, led by the resort's native warrior, Jomon. *$149–$199, $500–$1,000 suites. 11127 Front Beach Rd. (Hwy. 98), 32407, tel. 800/633–0266 or 850/234–1111, fax 850/235–1907, www.holidayinnsunspree.com. 337 rooms; 2 suites. Restaurant, in-room data ports, in-room safes, some in-room hot tubs, microwaves, refrigerators, cable TV, driving range, putting green, pool, gym, exercise equipment, hot tub, sauna, steam room, beach, 2 bars, children's programs (ages 3–18), laundry facilities, business services. AE, D, DC, MC, V.*

✪ **MARRIOTT'S BAY POINT RESORT VILLAGE** Across the Grand Lagoon from St. Andrews State Park, this expansive property exudes sheer elegance. The tropical-chic feel starts in the light-filled lobby, with its polished marble floors, glowing chandeliers, potted palms, and colorful floral paintings. Quiet guest rooms continue the theme with light wood furnishings and armoires, floral-print fabrics, and private balconies or patios overlooking the lush grounds and peaceful bay. Rooms on the upper floors of the main building have expansive views of the bay and the Gulf beyond, and kitchen-equipped villas are a mere tee-shot away from the hotel. A meandering boardwalk (which doubles as a jogging trail) leads to a private bayside beach where a seasonal open-air bar and water sports await. *$189–$219, $229 suites. 4200 Marriott Dr., 32408, tel. 800/874–7105 or 850/236–6000, fax 850/233–1308, www.marriottbaypoint.com. 278 rooms; 78 suites. 5 restaurants, some kitchens, cable TV, 2 18-hole golf courses, 4 pools, health club, marina, 2 bars, airport shuttle. AE, D, MC, V.*

MOONSPINNER CONDOMINIUM ♦ All the apartments in this resort are privately owned condominiums, but owners rent them when unoccupied. Each unit has two or three bedrooms, two bathrooms, a dining room, living room, kitchen, washer, dryer, dishwasher, and two decks with waterfront views, and sleeps up to eight people. Each condo is individually decorated; yearly renovations ensure a high standard of comfort. The resort is directly on the beach, adjacent to St. Andrew's State Park. *$120–$240. 4425 Thomas Dr., 32408, tel. 850/234–8900 or 800/223–3947, fax 850/ 233–0719, www.moonspinner.com. 162 units. Kitchenettes, microwaves, refrigerators, some in-room hot tubs, cable TV, in-room VCRs with movies, pool, wading pool, hot tub, 2 tennis courts, exercise equipment, beach, basketball, laundry facilities, business services. MC, V.*

MORE INFO

PANAMA CITY BEACH CONVENTION AND VISITORS BUREAU ♦ *17001 Panama City Beach Pkwy., Box 9473, Panama City Beach 32413, tel. 850/234–6575 or 800/722–3224, www.800pcbeach.com. Daily 9–5.*

GETTING HERE

Panama City Beach is on U.S. Highway 98, 21 mi southeast of Seaside, Florida. To get here from I–10, the main inland route, take U.S. Highway 231 south 50 mi to Panama City, then follow the signs over the causeway to the beaches.

PENSACOLA

In the years since its founding, Pensacola has come under the control of five nations, earning it the nickname the City of Five Flags. Spanish conquistadors landed on the shores of what is now Pensacola Bay in 1559, were driven away by storms, returned in 1698, then battled with French and British forces for control of the area throughout the 18th century. Finally, in 1821 Pensacola passed into U.S. hands with the rest of Florida—although during the Civil War it was governed by the Confederate States of America and flew yet another flag. As a result of this perpetual flag-swapping, the city has many historic sights, most of which are concentrated in Historic Pensacola's three districts—Seville, Palafox, and North Hill—which are easy to explore as a unit. Stroll down streets mapped out by the British and renamed by the Spanish, such as Cervantes, Palafox, Intendencia, and Tarragona. A recent influx of restaurants and bars is bringing new nightlife to the historic districts, but one-way streets can make navigating the area a bit tricky, especially at night.

SEE & DO

BIG LAGOON STATE RECREATION AREA ♦ This coastal park consists of 712 acres of sandy beaches and salt marshes. An observation tower gives you a bird's-eye view of local wildlife, including great blue herons and brown thrashers. Year-round camping is available, as well as swimming, fishing, boating, nature exhibits, guided walks, and campfire programs. *12301 Gulf Beach Hwy., 32507, tel. 850/492–1595, www.abfla.com/parks. $4 per vehicle. Daily 8 AM–dusk.*

✪ BLACKWATER RIVER STATE PARK In this 590-acre park the river, which starts in Alabama and flows downstream into Blackwater Bay, is supposedly one of the purest sandbottom rivers in the world. Its dark waters are in high contrast to the wide, white sandbars around the park. The terrain and plant life throughout the upland pine forest and open canopy forest is varied; you can camp, fish, canoe, and hike along nature trails here. *7720 Deaton Bridge Rd., 32564, tel. 850/983–5363, 800/326–3521 reservations, www.abfla.com/parks. $2 per vehicle. Daily 8 AM–dusk.*

CIVIL WAR SOLDIERS MUSEUM ♦ The collection here includes many items pertaining to Civil War medicine and an impressive collection of Civil War books. *108 S. Palafox Pl., 32501, tel. 850/469–1900, www.cwmuseum.org. $5. Tues.–Sat. 10–4:30.*

✪ FORT BARRANCAS Dating from the Civil War, the fort has picnic areas and a ½-mi woodland nature trail on its grounds. The fort is part of the Gulf Islands National Seashore, maintained by the National Park Service. *Bldg. #3822 NAS, Taylor Rd., tel. 850/455–5167. Free. Dec. and Jan., Wed.–Sun. 10:30–4; Feb.–Nov., daily 9:30–5.*

✪ HISTORIC PENSACOLA VILLAGE The Seville Square Historic District is the site of Pensacola's first permanent Spanish colonial settlement. Its center is Seville Square, a live oak–shaded park bounded by Alcaniz, Adams, Zaragoza, and Government streets. Within the Seville district is the Historic Pensacola Village, a complex of several museums, with indoor and outdoor exhibits that trace the area's history back 450 years. The Museum of Industry (200 E. Zaragoza St.), in a late 19th-century warehouse, hosts permanent exhibits dedicated to the lumber, maritime, and shipping industries—once mainstays of Pensacola's economy. A reproduction of a 19th-century streetscape is displayed in the Museum of Commerce (201 E. Zaragoza St.). Also in the village are the Julee Cottage (210 E. Zaragoza St.), Dorr House (311 S. Adams St.), Charles Lavallé House (205 E. Church St.), and Quina House (204 S. Alcaniz St.). Strolling through the area gives you a good look at many architectural styles, but to enter the museums you must purchase an all-inclusive ticket at the T. T. Wentworth Jr. Florida State Museum (included in the admission price) or the Village gift shop in the Tivoli House. *Tivoli House: 205 E. Zaragoza St., 32576-2866, tel. 850/595–5985, fax 850/595–5989, www.historicpensacola.org. $6, including Wentworth Museum. Weekdays 8–4:30.*

NATIONAL MUSEUM OF NAVAL AVIATION ◆ One of the world's largest air and space museums has 250,000 square feet of exhibit space and 27 acres of grounds. On display are more than 100 planes representing aviation in the Navy, the Marine Corps, and the Coast Guard at the Pensacola Naval Air Station. Among the planes are the NC-4, which in 1919 became the first plane to cross the Atlantic; the famous World War II fighter the F6 *Hellcat*; and the Skylab Command Module. On-site you'll also find aviators' mementos of historic battles, flight logs, vintage instruments, flight gear, a gift shop, a 14-seat flight simulator, and an IMAX theater playing *The Magic of Flight* and *Straight Up: Helicopters in Flight*. *1750 Radford Blvd., 32508, tel. 850/452–3604, 850/453–2024 IMAX theater, fax 850/452–3296, www.naval-air.org. Free, IMAX $6.50, Flight Simulator $3.50. Daily 9–5.*

NORTH HILL PRESERVATION DISTRICT ◆ Pensacola's affluent families, many made rich in the turn-of-the-20th-century timber boom, built their homes here where British and Spanish fortresses once stood. Residents still occasionally unearth cannonballs in their gardens. North Hill occupies 50 blocks, with more than 500 homes in Queen Anne, neoclassical, Tudor revival, and Mediterranean styles. Take a drive through this community, but remember these are private residences. Places of general interest include the 1902 Spanish mission–style **Christ Episcopal Church**; **Lee Square,** where a 50-foot obelisk stands as a tribute to the Confederacy; and **Fort George,** an undeveloped parcel at the site of the largest of three forts built by the British in 1778.

OLD PENSACOLA LIGHTHOUSE ♦ This is the tallest and oldest lighthouse in Florida, standing on a bluff overlooking Pensacola Pass, across Radford Boulevard from the National Museum of Naval Aviation. The 191-foot-high structure was built in 1858 after Andrew Jackson recommended that the area be used for a deep water naval station. Its first-order lens (a term designating its large size) was sent from Paris in 1924 and still guides ships and freighters. Climb the 178 steps to the top for a magnificent view. *Radford Blvd., 32508, tel. 850/455–2354. Free. Memorial Day–Labor Day, Sun. only, noon–4.*

PALAFOX HISTORIC DISTRICT ♦ Palafox Street is the main stem of the district, which was the commercial and government hub of Old Pensacola. Note the Spanish Renaissance–style **Saenger Theater,** Pensacola's old movie palace, and the **Bear Block,** a former wholesale grocery with wrought-iron balconies that are a legacy from Pensacola's Creole past. On Palafox between Government and Zaragoza streets is a **statue of Andrew Jackson** that commemorates the formal transfer of Florida from Spain to the United States in 1821. While in the area, stop by the **Wall South,** in Veterans Memorial Park, off Bayfront Parkway near 9th Avenue. The ¾-scale replica of the Vietnam Memorial in Washington, D.C., honors the more than 58,000 men and women who lost their lives in the Vietnam War.

PENSACOLA GREYHOUND TRACK ♦ Greyhound racing offers speedy dogs and the promise of fast money through pari-mutuel wagering. *951 Dog Track Rd., 32506, tel. 850/455–8595. $2. Wed.–Sat. 6 PM–10:30 PM, weekends 11–4.*

PENSACOLA MUSEUM OF ART ♦ Pensacola's city jail once occupied the 1906 Spanish revival–style building that is now the art museum. It provides a secure home for the museum's permanent collections of Oriental porcelain and works on paper by 20th-century artists; traveling exhibits range from photography to Dutch masters to works from local artists. *407 S. Jefferson St., 32502, tel. 850/432–6247, fax 850/469–1532, www.pensacolamuseumofart.org. $5, free Tues. Tues.–Fri. 10–5, weekends noon–5.*

ST. MICHAEL'S CEMETERY ♦ This late-18th-century cemetery contains 3,000 marked graves and monuments. *6 S. Alcaniz St. Free. Daily dawn–dusk.*

SCENIC HIGHWAY ♦ Atop the bluffs between Milton and Pensacola, Santa Rosa Island and Escambia Bay spread before you along this 20-mi stretch of U.S. 90. The best views are mostly between Nine Mile Road and 17th Avenue.

SHOP

Cordova Mall (5100 N. 9th Ave., tel. 850/477–5563), anchored by four department stores, has specialty shops and a food court.

OUTDOORS

Adventures Unlimited (Rte. 87, 12 mi north of Milton, tel. 850/623–6197 or 800/239–6864), on Coldwater Creek, rents light watercraft as well as campsites. Canoe season lasts roughly from March through mid-November. Canoe and kayak rentals for exploring the Blackwater River—the state's only sand-bottom river, and one of only three in the world—are available from **Blackwa-**

ter **Canoe Rental** (6974 Deaton Bridge Rd., Milton, tel. 850/623–0235 or 800/967–6789), northeast of Pensacola off I–10 Exit 10.

The **Moors** (3220 Avalon Blvd., Milton, tel. 850/994–2744), an 18-hole, par-70, Scottish links–style golf course, was designed by John LaFoy and is well known as the home of the Senior PGA Tour Emerald Coast Classic. The **Sportsman of Perdido** (1 Doug Ford Dr., tel. 850/492–1223) has a well-kept 18-hole golf course.

There are public tennis courts in more than 30 locations in the Pensacola area. The **Pensacola Racquet Club** (3450 Wimbledon Dr., tel. 850/434–2434) has 10 clay and 2 hard courts, plus a pool and restaurant.

Call **Rod and Reel Marina** (10045 Sinton Dr., tel. 850/492–0100), a mile west of Blue Angel Parkway off Gulf Beach Highway, to schedule a half- or full-day fishing charter. Bring your own food; the marina will supply everything else.

AFTER DARK

The **Pensacola Little Theatre** (400 S. Jefferson St., tel. 850/432–2042) presents plays and musicals year-round. **Pensacola's Symphony Orchestra** (tel. 850/435–2533) has 11 concerts each season at the Saenger Theatre. Productions at the restored 1926 **Saenger Theatre** (118 S. Palafox St., tel. 850/444–7686) include touring Broadway shows and three locally staged operas a year.

Emerald City (406 E. Wright St., tel. 850/433–9491) is a straight-friendly gay dance bar across from the Crowne Plaza hotel downtown. Nightly drink specials, karaoke nights, and drag performances keep the party going Wednesday through Monday. After dark, **McGuire's Irish Pub** (600 E. Gregory St., tel. 850/433–6789) welcomes those of Irish descent or anyone else who enjoys cold ale, beer, or lager. If you don't like crowds, stay away from McGuire's on Friday night and when Notre Dame games are televised. **Mesquite Charlie's** (5901 N. W St., 32505, tel. 850/434–0498) offers country music and all the western trappings. The **Seville Quarter** (130 E. Government St., 32501, tel. 850/434–6211), which has seven fabulous bars with music from disco to Dixieland, is Pensacola's equivalent of the New Orleans French Quarter.

EAT

✪ **DHARMA BLUE** On Seville Square, this trendy restaurant is a popular destination for lunch and dinner. A collection of southern folk art lends sly wit and exuberant color to the walls. A full sushi bar, cocktail bar, and inside and outside dining guarantee a pleasant wait for chef Andrea O'Bannon's creations. Daily specials vary with the season, but the regular luncheon menu includes choices like a grilled fresh salmon burger or a fried-green-tomato club sandwich. For dinner try sesame-crusted grouper with tempura-fried zucchini and sweet potatoes, cranberry glaze, and basmati rice. *$8–$28. 300 S. Alcaniz St., 32502, tel. 850/433–1275, www. dharmablue.com. AE, MC, V. No lunch Sun.*

JAMIE'S RESTAURANT ♦ An 1879 framed cottage in historic Pensacola was converted into this tiny restaurant. The cuisine is haute French, with light sauces and innovative flavor pairings. Start with a platter of smoked salmon and asparagus with a Dijon dill vinaigrette, or sautéed shrimp served on avocado with Cajun remoulade. For the main course, try roasted veal chop with shiitake mushroom and Madeira veal stock sauce or the black walnut-crusted rack of New Zealand lamb with caramelized pears and a port wine reduction sauce. *$25–$35. 424 E. Zaragoza St., 32502, tel. 850/434–2911. Reservations essential. AE, MC, V. Closed Sun.*

MESQUITE CHARLIE'S ♦ Saddle up and head on over to this Wild West saloon, with brick walls, arched doorways, mounted game, and a second-floor balcony overlooking the lobby. All that's missing are the swinging doors. The 32-ounce porterhouse is large enough to satisfy a posse of cowboys, but there are also smaller selections for dainty appetites. All are charbroiled with 100% mesquite charcoal and seasoned with natural spices. *$10–$29. 5901 N. W St., tel. 850/434–0498. AE, D, MC, V.*

MCGUIRE'S IRISH PUB ♦ Spend anywhere from $10 to $100 for a hamburger here, depending on whether you want it topped with cheddar or served with caviar and champagne. Beer is brewed on the premises, and the wine cellar has more than 8,000 bottles. Menu items range from Irish-style corned beef and cabbage to a hickory-smoked rib roast. In an old firehouse, the pub is replete with antiques, moose heads, Tiffany-style lamps, and Erin-go-bragh memorabilia. More than 250,000 dollar bills signed and dated by the pub's patrons flutter from the ceiling. *$5–$24. 600 E. Gregory St., tel. 850/433–6789, www.mcguiresirishpub.com. AE, D, MC, V.*

1912 RESTAURANT ♦ A converted 1912 train station houses this restaurant—with chandeliers, flowers, candles, low classical music, and dim lighting—which adjoins the soaring modern glass block of the Pensacola Grand Hotel. Specialties include steak, and a fish fillet broiled in white wine and butter, topped with crab and shrimp in a béarnaise sauce. *$12–$22. 200 E. Gregory St., 32501, tel. 850/433–3336, www.pensacolagrandhotel.com. AE, D, DC, MC, V. No dinner Sun.*

SKOPELOS ON THE BAY ♦ This 1959 restaurant, named after the Greek isle of the owners' birth, specializes in seafood, steak, veal, and lamb. A Grecian platter comes with moussaka, dolmades (stuffed vine leaves), spanakopita, lamb, and Greek salad. Scamp—a flaky, white deep water fish—is served with lump local blue crabmeat in a cream reduction. Grouper margarita comes breaded with a margarita sauce. Take in ocean views from the backyard patio deck, which rests 25 feet above the bay. *$14–$20. 670 Scenic Hwy., 32503, tel. 850/432–6565. AE, D, MC, V. Closed Sun. and Mon. No lunch Tues.–Thurs., Sat.*

SLEEP

BEST WESTERN VILLAGE INN ♦ This motel occupies four buildings around a courtyard pool. Some rooms have balconies or patios. The motel is across the street from West Florida Hospital, 4 mi from the airport, and 2 mi from West Florida University. *$49–$87. 8240 N. Davis Hwy., 32514, tel. 850/479–1099 or 888/879–3578, fax 850/479–9320, www.bwvillage.com. 142 rooms. Complimentary Continental breakfast, in-room data ports, some microwaves, some refrigerators, cable TV, pool, laundry service, business services. AE, D, DC, MC, V.*

CIVIC INN ♦ This white-stucco building with grey columns and royal blue doors had its origins as a 1950s travel lodge. It's a 10-minute walk from Pensacola's historic district and convenient to the trolley system, which you can use to get to museums and sights. *$36–$68. 200 N. Palafox St., 32501, tel. 850/432–3441, fax 850/438–5956. 48 rooms. Some microwaves, some refrigerators, cable TV, pool, laundry facilities, free parking, some pets allowed (fee). AE, D, MC, V.*

COMFORT INN ♦ This inn curls around a courtyard pool. There are rooms and two kinds of suites, which come with a refrigerator and microwave. It is 8 mi from downtown—take I–10 to Exit 13, then turn left. It's also within a half mile of University Mall. *$80–$90 doubles, $95 suites. 8080 N. Davis Hwy., 32514, tel. 850/484–8070 or 800/222–2222, fax 850/484–3853, www.comfortinn.com. 111 rooms; 4 suites. Complimentary Continental breakfast, in-room* *data ports, some microwaves, some refrigerators, cable TV, pool, exercise room, laundry service, laundry facilities, business services, airport shuttle, some pets allowed (fee). AE, D, DC, MC, V.*

COMFORT INN N.A.S.–CORRY ♦ This three-building motel is the entrance to Corry Field military base. The airport is 7 mi away, and the Historic District is 3 mi away. There are nearby hiking and jogging trails, fishing, and tennis facilities. *$67. 3 New Warrington Rd., 32506, tel. 850/455–3233 or 800/554–3206, fax 850/453–3445, www.choicehotels.com. 101 rooms. Complimentary Continental breakfast, in-room data ports, microwaves, refrigerators, cable TV, pool, bar, laundry facilities, business services, some pets allowed (fee). AE, D, DC, MC, V.*

✪ CROWNE PLAZA–PENSACOLA GRAND HOTEL The lobby of the former 1912 Louisville & Nashville train depot still has intact ticket and baggage counters, and old railroad signs remind you of the days when steam locomotives chugged up to these doors. A canopied two-story galleria leads to a 15-story tower—one of the tallest structures in town—where you leave the past behind and enjoy all the amenities of deluxe accommodations. Bi-level penthouse suites have snazzy wet bars and whirlpool baths. The hotel's proximity to downtown dining and nightlife, along with its amenities, makes it a good choice for business travelers. *$135, suites $250. 200 E. Gregory St., 32501, tel. 850/433–3336 or 800/348–3336, fax 850/432–7572, www.pensacolagrandhotel.com. 212 rooms; 8 suites. Restaurant, some in-room hot tubs, some minibars, cable TV, pool, gym, bar, library, business services, airport shuttle. AE, D, DC, MC, V.*

DAYS INN HISTORIC DOWNTOWN ♦ This motel was renovated in 2000. It's within an easy walk of restaurants, museums, art galleries, and shops and two blocks from the trolley stop. *$58–$100. 710 N. Palafox St., 32501, tel. 850/438–4922 or 800/544–8313, fax 850/438–7999, www.daysinn.com. 102 rooms. Restaurant, room service, in-room data ports, cable TV, outdoor pool, hair salon, bar, baby-sitting, laundry service, meeting rooms, some pets allowed (fee). AE, MC, V.*

ECONO LODGE ♦ This small, motel is 10 mi from the beach, 2 mi from University Mall, and 5 mi from the University of West Florida. Rooms, decorated in a contemporary style, come with either a queen or king bed. *$39–$49. 7194 Pensacola Blvd., 32505, tel. 850/479–8600 or 800/553–2666, fax 850/479–8600. 60 rooms. Complimentary Continental breakfast, cable TV, pool, laundry facilities, free parking. AE, D, DC, MC, V.*

FAIRFIELD INN MARRIOTT ♦ This motel is on the same block as University Mall, which has restaurants, shops, and a movie theater. West Florida University is 3 mi away, Marcus Point and Scenic Hills golf courses are 5 mi away, and the airport is 5 mi away. The executive rooms have pull-out beds, so you can sleep more than two people. *$69, executive rooms $79. 7325 N. Davis Hwy., 32514, tel. 850/484–8001 or 800/228–2800, fax 850/484–6008, www.marriott.com. 55 rooms; 8 executive rooms. Complimentary Continental breakfast, in-room data ports, some microwaves, some refrigerators, cable TV, indoor pool, business services. AE, D, DC, MC, V.*

HOLIDAY INN EXPRESS ♦ Palm trees rise around this three-story hotel at the entrance to University Mall. To reach it from I–10, get off at Exit 5 onto Highway 291, turn left at the bottom of the ramp and go on for ½ mi. The hotel is in the primary business district of Pensacola. The pool is shared with the Holiday Inn next door. *$69–$79. 7330 Plantation Rd., 32504, tel. 850/477–3333 or 800/426–7866, fax 850/477–8163, www.holiday-inn.com. 124 rooms. Complimentary Continental breakfast, in-room data ports, cable TV, pool, laundry service, business services, airport shuttle. AE, D, DC, MC, V.*

HOLIDAY INN UNIVERSITY MALL ♦ Next door to the Holiday Inn Express this two-story, four-building motel is also at the entrance to the University Mall in a commercial–business district of Pensacola. The motel offers reliable if unshowy quality, comfortable and clean rooms with nondescript furnishings, and of course convenient shopping opportunities. The hotel wraps around a shaded courtyard containing the pool. *$59–$100. 7200 Plantation Rd., 32504, tel. 850/474–0100 or 800/465–4329, fax 850/477–9821, www.holiday-inn.com. 152 rooms. Restaurant, in-room data ports, cable TV, pool, bar, laundry facilities, business services, airport shuttle. AE, D, MC, V.*

HOWARD JOHNSON EXPRESS INN ♦ This is a no-frills motel with basic, comfortable rooms, and a small breakfast area. The motel is 2 mi from downtown Pensacola and 1 mi from the Navy base. *$40–$100. 4126 Mobile Hwy., 32506, tel. 850/456–5731 or 800/406–1411, fax 850/456–5731, www.howardjohnson.com. 72 rooms. Complimentary Continental breakfast, microwaves, refrigerators, cable TV, pool. AE, D, DC, MC, V.*

LA QUINTA INN ♦ Like most properties in the La Quinta chain, this three-story motel has a white exterior with teal trim, and a sharp, vaguely Southwestern-style look. The beach and historic district are 7–8 mi away; the airport is 3 mi from the motel. *$70, suites $110. 7750 N. Davis Hwy., 32514-7557, tel. 850/474–0411 or 800/531–5900, fax 850/474–1521, www.laquinta.com. 128 rooms; 2 suites. Complimentary Continental breakfast, in-room data ports, some microwaves, some refrigerators, cable TV, pool, laundry facilities, some pets allowed. AE, D, DC, MC, V.*

LUXURY SUITES ♦ This inexpensive, family-owned all-suites hotel opened in 2000 with rooms in soothing peach, blue, and crimson touches. All rooms come with full kitchens, plus coffee machines, ironing boards, and pull-out love seats. The hotel is 1 mi off I–10 at Exit 3A. *$60–$97. 6703 Pensacola Blvd., 32505, tel. 850/484–5451, fax 850/484–4327, www.luxurysuitespensacola.com. 50 rooms. Complimentary Continental breakfast, in-room data ports, some in-room hot tubs, kitchenettes, minibars, microwaves, refrigerators, cable TV, pool, exercise equipment, laundry facilities, business services. AE, D, DC, MC, V.*

NEW WORLD INN ♦ If a small, warm, and cozy inn sounds appealing, this is the place for you. In the downtown historic area two blocks from Pensacola Bay, the inn contains furnishings that reflect the five periods of Pensacola's past: French and Spanish provincial, Early American, antebellum, and Queen Anne. Exquisite baths are handsomely appointed. *$75 for 1 person, $85 for 2 people, suite $125 for up to 2 people. 600 S. Palafox St., 32502, tel. 850/432–4111, fax 850/432–6836, www.newworldlanding.com. 14 rooms; 1 suite. Complimentary Continental breakfast, meeting rooms. AE, MC, V. CP.*

✪ PENSACOLA VICTORIAN This blue-grey Queen Anne home, complete with a turret and wraparound porch, was built for the ship captain William Northup, who later founded Pensacola's first philharmonic orchestra. The B&B has hardwood floors and paneling throughout. There's a stocked kitchen downstairs to which guests have access. The homemade breakfast includes fresh fruit salad, waffles, omelets or quiche, and homemade breads. The inn is only four blocks from the heart of downtown. Rooms don't have phones, but free phone outlets are available. *$75–$120. 203 W. Gregory St., 32501, tel. 800/370–8354, fax 850/429–0675, www.pensacolavictorian.com. 4 rooms. Complimentary breakfast, cable TV; no room phones, no smoking. AE, D, MC, V.*

RAMADA INN BAYVIEW ♦ This hotel, off I–10 at Exit 6, 5 mi from downtown, contains several buildings surrounding a landscaped courtyard with a pool and gazebo. The hotel, on a cliff overlooking the bay, offers Atlantic views from the restaurant and lounge. Rooms do not have water views. *$59–$90. 7601 Scenic Hwy., 32504, tel. 850/477–7155 or 800/212–1212, fax 850/477–7155, www.ramada.com. 150 rooms. Restaurant, complimentary Continental breakfast, in-room data ports, some microwaves, some refrigerators, cable TV, pool, hot tub, exercise equipment, bar, laundry service, laundry facilities, business services, airport shuttle, some pets allowed (fee). AE, D, DC, MC, V.*

RESIDENCE INN BY MARRIOTT ♦ In the downtown bay-front area, this all-suites hotel is perfect for extended stays, whether for business or pleasure. The location is ideal for exploring Pensacola's historic streets on foot, and families will especially appreciate the fully equipped kitchens and free grocery delivery. Breakfast and evening social hour are complimentary. *$119–$185. 601 E. Chase St., 32502, tel. 850/432–0202, fax 850/438–7965, www. residenceinn.com. 78 suites. Kitchens, some microwaves, some refrigerators, cable TV, tennis court, pool, gym, basketball, some pets allowed (fee). AE, D, DC, MC, V.*

MORE INFO

The best way to orient yourself is to stop at the **Pensacola Visitor Information Center,** at the foot of the Pensacola Bay Bridge. Pick up good maps of the city here. *1401 E. Gregory St., 32502, tel. 850/ 434–1234 or 800/874–1234, www.visitpensacola.com. Weekdays 8–5, weekends 9–4.*

GETTING HERE

Pensacola is at the western end of the Florida Panhandle, about 15 mi east of the Alabama border. To get here from I–10 inside Florida, simply head west and follow the signs: I–10 passes directly through Pensacola before heading on to points west. To get here from the Gulf beaches, follow U.S. Highway 98 east to Pensacola Beach and follow the signs to the Pensacola Bay Bridge.

PENSACOLA BEACH

The skinny barrier island of Santa Rosa has beaches, natural areas, and the tourist town of Pensacola Beach. Truth be told, most of the culture—as well as most of the good restaurants—in the greater Pensacola area is found on the mainland, so you're better off heading to the beaches for gorgeous seascapes, myriad water sports, miles of cycling trails, and prime bird-watching (more than 280 species of birds have been spotted here). Two caveats for visitors: "Leave nothing behind but your footprints" and—enforced by mighty big fines—"Don't pick the sea oats," the natural grasses that help keep the dunes intact. You should also mind the speed limit when passing through the town of Gulf Breeze on the way to the beach—the police there are famous for handing out unwelcome souvenirs of their own.

SEE & DO

✪ **GULF ISLANDS NATIONAL SEASHORE** Dotting the 150-mi stretch between Destin and Gulfport, Mississippi, the Gulf Islands National Seashore is managed by the National Park Service. Many good beach and recreational spots are part of the national seashore along this beautiful stretch of island coast. Although the park is open year-round, there are seasonal restrictions, so call ahead. At

Opal Beach Day Use Area (Rte. 399, 5 mi east of Pensacola Beach) you'll find pristine coastline, barbecue areas, covered picnic facilities, and rest rooms. At the western tip of the island and part of the Gulf Islands National Seashore, **Fort Pickens** dates to 1834. Constructed of more than 21 million locally made bricks, the fort once served as the prison of Apache chief Geronimo. A National Park Service plaque describes the complex as a "confusing jumble of fortifications," but the real attractions here are the beach, nature exhibits, a large campground, an excellent gift shop, and breathtaking views of Pensacola Bay and the lighthouse across the inlet. It's the perfect place for a picnic lunch and a bit of history, too. *Ft. Pickens Rd., tel. 850/934–2635. $8 per car. Daily 7 AM–dusk.*

USS *MASSACHUSETTS* ◆ You can find this 1896 battleship—the oldest such American vessel—26 feet under the Gulf of Mexico in the Fort Pickens State Aquatic Preserve, 1½ mi south-southwest of Pensacola Pass. Following its decommission in 1919, the USS *Massachusetts* was used for artillery practice. Today, the ship is an artificial reef popular with divers, its 350-foot hulk partially buried in a white sandy bottom. *Tel. 850/434–1234, dhr.dos.state.fl.us/bar/uap.*

PENSACOLA BEACH GULF PIER ◆ The 1,471-foot-long pier bills itself as the longest pier on the Gulf of Mexico. Serious anglers will find everything they'll need—from pole rentals to bait—to land that big one, but those looking to catch only a beautiful sunset are welcome, too. Check the pier's Web site for the latest fishing reports on what's biting. *41 Fort Pickens Rd., tel. 850/934–7200, fax 850/916–7900, www.fishpensacolabeachpier.com. Observers $1, fishing $6.50.*

OUTDOORS

For a full- or half-day deep-sea charter ($75–$95 per person), try the **Beach Marina** (655 Pensacola Beach Blvd., tel. 850/932–8466), which represents several charters.

When you rent a sailboat, Jet Ski, or catamaran from **Bonifay Water Sports** (460 Pensacola Beach Blvd., 32561, tel. 850/932–0633, AE, D, MC, V), you'll also receive safety and sailing instructions. There's also a 24-foot pontoon boat—perfect for a picnic cruise down the Intracoastal—for rent, as well as go-karts and a minigolf course.

The **Club at Hidden Creek** (3070 PGA Blvd., Navarre 32563, tel. 850/939–4604) is a semiprivate 18-hole course.

EAT

✪ **FLOUNDER'S CHOWDER AND ALE HOUSE** Combine a Gulf-front view at this casual restaurant with a fruity tropical libation, and you're all set for a night of "floundering" at its best. This family-friendly spot has a playground and game room, and the eclectic collection of antiques and objets d'art creates a fun, funky atmosphere. The house specialty is seafood charbroiled over a hardwood fire, but the extensive menu offers several choices for those who don't love fish. After dinner, dance beneath the stars at the Key West–style beach bar. *$4–$25. 800 Quietwater Beach Blvd., 32508, tel. 850/932–2003. AE, D, DC, MC, V.*

✪ **JUBILEE** Topside is the formal half of this restaurant complex, with stained glass, antiques, 1930s photographs of Pensacola, and a view of Quietwater Sound. The menu here has dishes such as smoked Gouda shrimp, Cajun-fried artichoke hearts, carrot raisin Ahi, and soft shell crabs with honey-roasted nuts. Downstairs, a more casual café called Beachside serves sandwiches of such items as BBQ chicken and fried oysters. There's live entertainment on the weekends. Beachside: reservations not accepted. Topside: reservations essential. *$7–$25. 400 Quietwater Beach Rd., 32561, tel. 850/934–3108, fax 850/932–0046, www.jubileefun.com. AE, D, DC, MC, V.*

PEG LEG PETE'S OYSTER BAR ♦ This funky, fun place—there's a volleyball court and gift shop on the ground level—overlooks LaFitte Cove Marina. You can bring your boat and dock behind the restaurant. Try the fried grouper or the chargrilled mahimahi. There is a kids' menu. *$5–$18. 1010 Fort Pickens Rd., 32561, tel. 850/932–4139, fax 850/932–1077, www.peglegpetes.com. AE, MC, V.*

SLEEP

✪ **BEST WESTERN RESORT PENSACOLA BEACH** This modern, two-building complex on the beach is in the middle of the Pensacola Beach nightlife scene. On the bay side, you can go parasailing, and rent boats and jet skis. Each room comes with a full kitchen, 27-inch TV, coffeemakers, hair dryers, and ironing boards. *$79–$250. 16 Via De Luna, Pensacola Beach 32561, tel. 850/934–3300 or 800/934–3301, fax 850/934–9780, www.bestwestern.com. 123 rooms. Complimentary Continental breakfast, in-room data ports, minibars, microwaves, refrigerators, cable TV, 2 pools, beach, boating, bar, playground, laundry facilities, business services. AE, D, DC, MC, V.*

✪ **COMFORT INN PENSACOLA BEACH** One of the best deals on the beach, this well-kept chain motel sits on the bay side overlooking Little Sabine Bay, but the upper floors have views of the Gulf just across the street. Breezy, floral-print fabrics and rattan furnishings lend a cheeriness to the guest rooms. Free local phone calls seal the deal. Restaurants and shops are within walking distance. *$80–$180. 40 Fort Pickens Rd., 32561, tel. 850/934–5400 or 800/934–5470, fax 850/934–7210, www.comfortinn.com. 99 rooms. Complimentary Continental breakfast, picnic area, microwaves, refrigerators, cable TV, pool, volleyball, meeting rooms. AE, D, DC, MC, V. CP.*

THE DUNES ♦ All rooms face the Gulf of Mexico with private balconies in this eight-story, U-shape complex directly on the beach.

Except for four one-bedroom penthouses, all units are simple studios. *$150. 333 Fort Pickens Rd., Pensacola Beach 32561, tel. 850/932–3536 or 800/833–8637, fax 850/932–7088, www.theduneshotel.com. 76 rooms. Restaurant, room service, in-room data ports, in-room safes, some in-room hot tubs, some minibars, some refrigerators, cable TV, outdoor pool, massage, beach, bar, baby-sitting, laundry service. AE, D, MC, V.*

HAMPTON INN PENSACOLA BEACH ♦ The exterior's pink-and-green color scheme is reminiscent of Miami Beach's art deco buildings, and the easygoing Florida style continues inside. Directly on the Gulf and centrally located, this lodging is within walking distance of several popular restaurants and shops. Most rooms have a Gulf view, and all are oversize. Gulf-front rooms have private balconies. There's an evening cocktail hour, and an expansive Continental breakfast buffet is served. *$89–$199. 2 Via de Luna, Pensacola Beach 32561, tel. 850/932–6800 or 800/320–8108, fax 850/932–6833, www.hamptonbeachresort.com. 181 rooms. Microwaves, refrigerators, cable TV with movies, 2 pools, gym, beach, bar. AE, D, DC, MC, V. CP.*

PERDIDO SUN ♦ This high-rise is the perfect expression of Gulf-side resort living. One-, two-, and three-bedroom decorator-furnished condos all have seaside balconies with spectacular water views. Choose to make this your home away from home—accommodations include fully equipped kitchens—or pamper yourself with daily maid service. *$90–$150. 13753 Perdido Key Dr., Perdido Key 32507, tel. 850/492–2390 or 800/227–2390, fax 850/492–4125, www.perdidosun.com. 93 condos. Cable TV with movies, 2 pools, gym, beach. AE, D, MC, V.*

SABINE YACHT AND RACQUET CLUB ♦ This family-run, high-rise offers balconies that run the length of each one- or two-bedroom unit. Rooms have views of Little Sabine Bay in back or the Gulf of Mexico in front, across the street. All units come with full-size kitchen and sleeper sofas. *$155–$190. 330 Ft. Pickens Rd.,*

32561, tel. 850/932–7290 or 800/343–0344, fax 850/932–7647, www.sabinecondo.com. 81 units. Picnic area, some in-room hot tubs, kitchenettes, microwaves, refrigerators, cable TV, 2 tennis courts, pool, exercise equipment, sauna, beach, dock, boating, fishing, laundry facilities. AE, D, MC, V.

MORE INFO

PENSACOLA BEACH CHAMBER OF COMMERCE ♦ *735 Pensacola Beach Blvd., Pensacola Beach 32561, tel. 800/635–4803, fax 850/932–1551, www.pensacolabeachchamber.org.*

GETTING HERE

Pensacola Beach is about 5 mi south of Pensacola via U.S. 98. Take the 3-Mile Bridge heading south out of town to Route 399 in Gulf Breeze. Follow the signs to the beach via the Bob Sikes Bridge. The 3-Mile Bridge is free, but there's a $1 toll for the Bob Sikes Bridge.

PERRY

The Florida National Scenic Trail runs 17 mi south of this rural community of 7,000. The surrounding area is thickly wooded; camping, fishing, and hiking are popular. The Forest Capital State Museum explores the history of the local forest industry. One of the area's major industries—and an up-and-coming tourist draw—is scalloping, which is allowed only during the official harvesting months of July, August, and the early part of September. Perry is also home to the Florida Forest Festival (call 850/584–8733 for information), a month-long October event that offers everything from lumberjack shows to arts and crafts displays to the "World's Largest Free Fish Fry."

SEE & DO

✪ **FOREST CAPITAL STATE MUSEUM AND CRACKER HOMESTEAD**
Long-leaf pines grow on the 13-acre grounds of this museum and homestead, which celebrates the local timber industry and early settlers. Inside the museum, exhibit cases are made of different native woods, including redwood, ash, and magnolia. A 5-foot map of Florida outlines the state's 67 counties with 67 different types of local wood. The exhibits cover timber issues past and present, from animal species in hammock areas to reasons for prescribed

burning. The Cracker Homestead is the best remaining example of a dog trot–style of housing favored by early settlers, who were called "crackers" for their use of the bull whip in cattle driving. The house features big porches, with a breezeway running through the house leading to a backyard kitchen. The complex is 1 mi south of town. *204 Forest Park Dr., 32347, tel. 850/584–3227, fax 850/584–3488. $1. Thurs.–Mon. 9–noon, 1–5.*

✪ **LAFAYETTE BLUE SPRINGS** Also known as Mayo Blue Springs, these crystal clear springs are on the Suwannee River, 20 mi southeast of Perry along U.S. 27. You can swim, picnic, hike along nature trails, and use the boat ramps. *Hwy. 27 Exit 251b, Mayo 32066. $1.50. Weekdays 8:30–8:30, weekends 8–8:30.*

EAT

✪ **DOWNTOWN CAFÉ OF PERRY** This Main Street restaurant is in the middle of other shops and cafés, but people come here for the all-you-can-eat $5.99 buffet, featuring heavy country biscuits, fried chicken, pork chops, soups, and salads. Hamburgers are the biggest sellers. *$6–$8. 108 E. Main St., 32347, tel. 850/584–2232. MC, V. Closed weekends; no dinner Mon.–Thurs.*

POUNCEY'S RESTAURANT ♦ This comfortable restaurant has a friendly staff and down-home menu classics like country-fried steak and fried chicken. Servings are generous and the prices are low. *$7–$12. 2186 S. Byron Butler Pkwy., tel. 850/584–9942. No credit cards.*

SLEEP

PERRY DAYS INN ♦ This small two-story motel is in the center of rural Perry and is a popular place to stay if you're in the area for fishing or hunting. *$49–$56. 2277 S. Byron Butler Pkwy., 32348, tel. 850/584–5311 or 800/544–8313, fax 850/584–5311, www.daysinn. com. 60 rooms. Some in-room data ports, in-room safes, some microwaves, some refrigerators, cable TV, pool, laundry service, some pets allowed (fee). AE, D, DC, MC, V.*

SOUTHERN INN ♦ This basic motel is surrounded by fast-food chains and a retail area with a huge laundromat. This two-story redbrick building takes up only a portion of the 4 acres it owns, so there's a touch of nature around. While not big on charm, you can't beat the price. The place fills up quickly in the fall during Florida State University college football weekends. *$35–$45. 2238 S. Byron Butler Pkwy., 32347, tel. 850/584–4221, fax 850/838–1718. 66 rooms. Complimentary Continental breakfast, some kitchenettes, some microwaves, some refrigerators, cable TV, pool, some pets allowed (fee). AE, MC, V.*

MORE INFO

PERRY-TAYLOR COUNTY CHAMBER OF COMMERCE ♦ *428 N. Jefferson St., Box 892, Perry 32347, tel. 850/584–5366, fax 850/584– 8030, www.taylorcountychamber.com.*

GETTING HERE

Perry lies at the Florida Panhandle's eastern extreme, at the intersection of U.S. 98 and U.S. 19 (also known as Alternate U.S. 27 as it continues south). To reach Perry from I–10, take U.S. 19 south about 40 mi.

SEASIDE

This community of Victorian-style homes is so reminiscent of a storybook town that producers chose it for the set of the 1998 film *The Truman Show*, starring Jim Carrey. The brainchild of Robert Davis, the town was designed to promote a neighborly, old-fashioned lifestyle, and there's much to be said for an attractive, billboard-free village where you can park your car and walk everywhere you need to go. Pastel-color homes with white picket fences, front-porch rockers, and captain's walks are set amid red-brick streets, and all are within walking distance of the town center and its unusual cafés and shops. Seaside's popularity continues to soar, and the summer months can be crowded. If you're seeking a little solitude, you might prefer visiting during the off-season—between Labor Day and Memorial Day.

SHOP

Seaside's central square and open-air market, along Route 30A, offer a number of unique and whimsical boutiques carrying clothing, jewelry, and arts and crafts. **Perspicasity** (Rte. 30A, Santa Rosa Beach, tel. 850/231–5829, fax 850/231–5496), an open-air market in Santa Rosa Beach, sells simply designed women's clothing and accessories perfect for easy, carefree beach-town casualness.

Ruskin Place Artist Colony (tel. 800/277–8696, Apr.–Oct., daily 10–7; Nov.–Mar., daily 10–5), in the heart of Seaside, is a quaint collection of galleries and craft shops.

OUTDOORS

An 8-foot-wide pathway covering 18 mi of scenic Route 30A winds past freshwater lakes, woodlands, and beaches. **Butterfly Rentals** (3657 E. Rte. 30A, tel. 850/231–2826) rents bikes and kayaks and has free delivery and pickup. In Seaside, consult the **Cabana Man** (tel. 850/231–5046) for beach chairs, umbrellas, rafts, kayaks, and anything else you might need for a day at the beach. If there's no answer, just head to the beach and you'll find him there.

EAT

BUD & ALLEY'S ♦ This beachside bistro has been a local favorite since 1986. Indoors are hardwood floors, ceiling fans, and 6-foot windows looking onto an herb garden; the roof-top Tarpon Club bar makes a great perch for a sunset toast. A porch provides the perfect spot for admiring the orange sunsets common in the fall. Daily salad specials are tangy introductions to such entrées as sesame-seared rare tuna on wild greens with a rice-wine vinaigrette and a soy dipping sauce. *$19–$30. 2236 E. Rte. 30A, Seaside, tel. 850/231–5900. MC, V. Closed Tues. and Jan.*

✪ CAFE THIRTY-A In a beautiful Florida-style home with high ceilings and a wide veranda, this restaurant has an elegant look—bolstered by white linen tablecloths—and impeccable service. The menu changes nightly and includes such entrées as lemon-marinated salmon, oven-roasted black grouper, and braised Arizona rabbit. Even if you're not a Southerner, you should try the appetizer of grilled Georgia quail with creamy grits and sage fritters. With nearly 20 creative varieties, the martini menu alone is worth the trip. *$21–$35. 3899 E. Rte. 30A, Seagrove Beach 32459, tel. 850/231–2166. AE, D, DC, MC, V. No lunch.*

SHADES ♦ This is the most relaxed of Seaside's restaurants—kids' dishes come served on a Frisbee—and you can get a good half-pound burger here, beside a variety of fresh fish, calamari, salads, and other inexpensive fare. Perhaps Shades is best known for its homemade seafood sauces, including a Jack Daniels tangy mustard sauce for grouper and dolphin (mahimahi) fish bites, and a sweet barbecue sauce for shrimp. Outdoor dining is available in a big deck outside this converted century-old house. *$10–$19. 83 Central Sq., Santa Rosa Beach 32459, tel. 850/231–1950. Reservations not accepted. AE, MC, V.*

SLEEP

JOSEPHINE'S FRENCH COUNTRY INN ♦ The charming rooms in this grand, Georgian-style accommodation have Gulf views, four-poster beds, fireplaces, and claw-foot tubs, bringing a bit of elegance to a modern seaside spot. The daily country-style breakfast is delicious, and dinners are garnished with fresh herbs and flowers from the owners' garden. *$200–$250. 38 Seaside Ave., 32459, tel. 800/848–1840 or 850/231–1940, fax 850/231–2446, www.josephinesinn.com. 7 rooms; 2 suites. Microwaves, refrigerators, in-room VCRs. AE, D, MC, V. EP.*

✪ SEASIDE COTTAGE RENTAL AGENCY When residents aren't using their homes, they rent out their one- to six-bedroom, porticoed, faux-Victorian cottages—a perfect option for a family vacation or a large group. Gulf breezes blowing off the water remind you of the unspoiled sugar-white beaches a short stroll away. *$333–$1,231. Rte. 30A, Box 4730, 32459, tel. 850/231–1320 or 800/277–8696, fax 850/231–2373, www.seasidefl.com. 300 units. Kitchens,* *cable TV, in-room VCRs, 6 tennis courts, 3 pools, bicycles, badminton, croquet. AE, D, MC, V.*

✪ **WATERCOLOR INN** Nature meets seaside chic at this new boutique property, the crown jewel of the area's latest—and largest—planned community. Rooms are done in seashell tones with vibrant, sea-blue comforters and accents; stylish armoires and desks look as natural and unfinished as driftwood. Dune-level bungalows have private courtyards with outdoor showers, while upper rooms have huge balconies and walk-in showers with windows overlooking the Gulf. Standard rooms come with a king-size bed and a queen sleeper-sofa, but consider one of the three Rotunda rooms for something larger and more spectacular. *$289–$315. 34 Goldenrod Circle, Seagrove Beach 32459, tel. 850/534–5000, fax 850/534–5001, www.watercolorinn.com. 42 rooms. Restaurant, fans, in-room data ports, in-room safes, minibars, cable TV, golf privileges, pool, outdoor hot tub, massage, beach, library, Internet, airport shuttle, no-smoking rooms. AE, D, MC, V.*

MORE INFO

SEASIDE COMMUNITY DEVELOPMENT CORPORATION ♦ *Box 4730, Seaside 32459, tel. 800/277–8696, www.seasidefl.com.*

GETTING HERE

Seaside is on Route 30A, also known as Scenic Route 30A, 20 mi east of Destin and 25 mi west of Panama City via U.S. 98. Part of what gives the community its old-fashioned "seaside" charm is that U.S. 98, which runs through the middle of most every other Gulf-front community in these parts, runs farther inland here, saving Seaside from the constant rumble of traffic—and the eyesores of fast food joints and strip malls.

ST. JOSEPH PENINSULA

If you're looking for towering sand dunes and utter quiet on your beach vacation, this is the place. Tucked away far from Panama City Beach's maddening crowds (but close enough to take day trips with the kids), St. Joseph Peninsula and its environs are delightfully rural and close to nature.

Ironically, in an earlier time, this was one of the state's fastest growing areas. Then, in 1841, twin disasters struck. A sailing ship from the West Indies introduced yellow fever to the area. It spread quickly, and the epidemic, combined with a powerful hurricane, wiped the original settlement of St. Joseph off the map.

The first Cape San Blas lighthouse, built in 1847, made St. Joseph Peninsula an important Civil War site. Salt was processed nearby from the sea to supply the Confederate army. Since then, three more lighthouses have been constructed to replace those swallowed by the sea as the narrow peninsula shifted.

Today, the 22-mi crook of land with its ivory colored sands offers beachgoers exciting vistas and natural habitats capped by the 2,500-acre St. Joseph Peninsula State Park, whose beach was ranked best in the United States in 2003 by Dr. Steven Leatherman, a coastal biologist better known as "Dr. Beach." Driving from the mainland, you'll find a fragile stretch of sand so narrow that you can see both the Gulf of Mexico and St. Joseph Bay from the road nearly all the time. Scrubby vegetation pokes through the high dunes.

The casually organized community on the peninsula is known as Cape San Blas, for the chin of land jutting into the Gulf at the southern end. Most residents are seasonal. The community subsists on tourism, but it's low key. You won't find everything you need here, and that's part of the charm. A vacation on the peninsula requires that you get out and explore the wilderness and fishing towns around it. Port St. Joe, a once-odiferous paper-mill port town, has cleaned up its act of late and is poised to capitalize on its proximity to such spectacular natural environs (the paper mill was razed in 2002 to make way for a luxury condo development). The town offers an unusual range of water activities, including world-class wreck diving—the hulk of the *Empire Mica*, a British tanker torpedoed in World War II, is one of the best underwater sights in the Panhandle. You can also harvest your own scallops here. (It's one of the few places in Florida where the public can do so, thanks to plentiful supplies.)

Visitors often venture as far as Panama City to the west and Apalachicola to the east for dining and entertainment, but they return gratefully to the eerie silence of Cape San Blas. Here you'll find hawks, peregrine falcons, foxes, and armadillos. Come fall, the beach may be covered with migrating monarch butterflies. Beach time is a quiet affair that allows you to commune with the cosmos, dig your toes into soft, fine sand, and take occasional dips in water that maintains a temperature range of between 64 and 83 degrees.

SEE & DO

CAPE SAN BLAS ♦ This peninsula is nothing but sand, so the beach is rarely more than a few steps away. Tall dunes rise from the wide beach apron, and the sands spread wide and luxuriously fine, with scatterings of coquinas and other small shells at the water's edge. **Salinas Park** (Rte. 30 E, near the intersection of Rte. 30) is a great little beach park, but you may have to share it with the mosquitoes in the summertime if the wind is off the bay. Also, beware of stepping on sand spurs (burry seed pods). The beach is wide here and hard-packed near the clear, green water. You'll see a lot of ghost crabs and their holes. There are picnic tables and a nice playground. Boardwalks lead to the beach and to a breezy gazebo at the top of one dune. There are no lifeguards here.

CONSTITUTION CONVENTION MUSEUM STATE PARK ♦ In a park setting, a monument and museum commemorate Florida's first state Constitution Convention in 1838 and relate other facts of local history. *200 Allen Memorial Way, Port St. Joe, tel. 850/229–8029, www.floridastateparks.org/constitutionconvention. Thurs.–Mon. 9–noon and 1–5. $1.*

ST. JOSEPH CEMETERY ♦ While visiting the Constitution Convention Museum, stop by this site, which holds the remains of the area's first settlers. *Garrison Ave., Port St. Joe.*

✪ **ST. JOSEPH PENINSULA STATE PARK** The view from the boardwalk tells you that you've come to the right place. Tall dunes make you feel hidden from the world, and the fine sand seems to stretch endlessly in either direction. Except for an occasional jet from the local Air Force base, there's no hint of civilization. The swimming is good here; expect gently sloping sand and refreshingly cool water with small, playful breakers. Rest rooms and showers are off the boardwalk. Across the road are a park store, picnic shelters, and a playground. Not far outside the park entrance, there's a restaurant and a general store. The park boat basin has canoe rentals and a boat ramp and there's surf-casting in the Gulf and fishing in St. Joseph Bay. Note that there are no lifeguards here. To get here exit U.S. Highway 98 at Route 30 E and follow it to the end of St. Joseph Peninsula. *8899 Cape San Blas Rd., 32456, tel. 850/227–1327. $3.25 per car. Daily 8 AM–dusk.*

SHOP

Cape Tradin' Post (4975 Cape San Blas Rd., Cape San Blas 32456, tel. 850/229–8775), along with two other convenience stores, provides the only shopping on the peninsula. Here you'll find groceries, beach necessities, toys, and T-shirts.

You can get good fresh produce at **Piggly Wiggly** (125 W. U.S. Hwy. 98, Port St. Joe 32456, tel. 850/229–8398).

OUTDOORS

Divers have plenty to explore in these waters. There are a dozen or so wrecks offshore, and lots of colorful fish hang out around the brick base of a former lighthouse at Cape San Blas. **Daily Stock Dive Shop** (Hwy. 98, Port St. Joe, tel. 850/229–6330) arranges dive charters and teaches certification courses.

One of the few places in Florida where the public may harvest scallops (the season runs from July through August), St. Joseph Bay has lots of good fishing. To try deeper waters, you can catch a boat out of Mexico Beach or Port St. Joe. **Pics Food Store** (Rte. 30 E, Cape San Blas, tel. 904/227–1897) sells fishing and scalloping supplies and licenses.

The quiet roads of Cape San Blas are ideal for biking, but bring your own. There are no bike rentals in the vicinity.

St. Joseph's Bay Country Club (700 Country Club Rd., Port St. Joe 32456, tel. 850/227–1751, www.sjbcc.com) has a clubhouse, restaurant, and 18 holes open to nonmembers.

St. Joseph Peninsula has a public boat ramp. It also rents canoes for use in the park. **St. Joe Boat Rentals** (Simmons Bayou, Port St. Joe, tel. 904/229–6585) rents 14-foot powerboats and pontoon boats. From Route 30 E, turn left on C-30 and go 6 mi.

Cape San Blas has no public tennis courts, but there are three in Port St. Joe: one in Frank Pate Park on Highway 98 at 5th Street, and two on 8th Street.

EAT

INDIAN PASS RAW BAR ♦ Housed in an old roadside general store, this place is famous for its gumbo, oysters, steamed shrimp, clams, crawfish, and local color. It's 2 mi east of the 30 E turn-off to Cape San Blas. *$5–$17. Rte. 30 B, Port St. Joe, tel. 850/227–1670, www.indianpassrawbar.com. AE, D, MC, V.*

✪ **TOUCAN'S** It's a bit out of the way (25 minutes from St. Joseph Peninsula), but it's one of the best places in the vicinity. Besides, it has a beach, so bring the family and go for lunch and some sun. An extensive menu emphasizes seafood. Have oysters raw, steamed, or baked eight different ways. Bourbon Street snapper (baked in cajun seasonings) and seafood mustafa (shrimp, lobster, or blue crab with vegetables and a light cream sauce) are winners. Note that breakfast is served in summer only. *$15–$17. 812 Hwy. 98, Mexico Beach 32410, tel. 850/648–8207, fax 850/648–3010. AE, D, MC, V.*

SLEEP

Lodging in Cape San Blas once consisted of campsites and cabins. Now, residential and resort communities offer other accommodations at reasonable rates.

Cape San Blas also has a nice selection of rental homes and town houses. Weekly rates run from $600 for a cottage to $3,000 for a deluxe, multibedroom home. Contact **Anchor Realty & Mortgage Co** (6260 Hwy. 98, Port St. Joe 32456, tel. 800/411–3717, fax 850/229–1174, www.florida-beach.com) for listings. **Cape San Blas Realty** (4320 Cape San Blas Rd., Port St. Joe 32456, tel. 850/229–6916, fax 850/229–8783, www.capesanblasvacationrentals.com) has listings for rentals.

✪ **OLD SALT WORKS CABINS** A Civil War historic site and museum add interest to these pleasant, privately owned cabins, which front either Gulf or bay and offer a real back-to-nature experience. In Fort Crooked Tree, children can play with mannequins in Civil War dress. The cabins are on the bay side shortly after you turn onto the Cape on Route 30 E. *$79–$119. 1085 Cape San Blas, Port St. Joe 32456, tel. 850/229–6097, www.oldsaltworks.com. 11 cabins. MC, V.*

ST. JOSEPH PENINSULA STATE PARK ♦ Besides tent and RV sites, there are eight furnished town house–style cabins that are clearly not your average rustic state park lodging. Cabins sleep up to seven and each has a fireplace, screened porch, and boardwalk leading to the bay. Guests are asked to bring extra towels. Reserve well in advance. Check in at the park is from 8 AM to sunset. The entrance is on St. Joseph Peninsula, at the end of Route 30 E. *Tent/RV sites $15 plus $2 for electricity, cabins $70, Star Rte. 1, Box 200, Port St. Joe 32456, tel. 850/227–1327 or 800/326–3521 for reservations, www.reservamerica.com. 8 cabins.*

MORE INFO

GULF COUNTY CHAMBER OF COMMERCE ♦ *104 4th St. W, Port St. Joe 32456 (Box 964, Port St. Joe 32457), tel. 850/227–1223, www.gulfcountybusiness.com. Weekdays 8–5.*

GETTING HERE

From Panama City Regional Airport (an hour from St. Joseph Peninsula State Park), take Airport Road to U.S. Highway 98 and turn left. Follow Highway 98 east of Port St. Joe to Route C-30 (about 40 mi). Turn right and follow signs for St. Joseph Peninsula State Park. The signs will direct you to turn right on Route 30 E to Cape San Blas.

ST. GEORGE ISLAND

Pristine St. George Island sits 5 mi out into the Gulf of Mexico just south of Apalachicola. Accessed via the Bryant Patton Bridge off U.S. 98, the island is bordered by both Apalachicola Bay and the Gulf, offering vacationers the best of both. The rich bay is an angler's dream, while the white beaches and clear Gulf waters satisfy even the most finicky beachgoer. Indulge in bicycling, hiking, canoeing, and snorkeling or find a secluded spot for reading, gathering shells, or bird-watching. Accommodations mostly take the form of privately owned, fully furnished condos and single-family homes, which allow for plenty of privacy.

SEE & DO

✪ **ST. GEORGE ISLAND STATE PARK** This is Old Florida at its undisturbed best. On the east end of the island are 9 mi of undeveloped beaches and dunes—the longest beachfront of any state park in Florida. Sandy coves, salt marshes, oak forests, and pines provide shelter for many species, including such birds as bald eagles and ospreys. Spotless rest rooms and plentiful parking make a day at this park a joy. *1900 E. Gulf Beach Dr., 32328, tel. 850/927–2111, fax 850/927–2500, www.floridastateparks.org/stgeorgeisland. $4 per vehicle, up to 8 people. Daily 8 AM–dusk.*

CARRABELLE ◆ Where, exactly, is Carrabelle? Why, it's between Sopchoppy and Wewahitchka, of course. Known locally as "a quaint drinking village with a fishing problem," one of the last true fishing ports on the Gulf Coast is most famous for having the World's Smallest Police Station, a former phone booth off U.S. 98 (you can buy the postcard at the nearby general store). Talk a walk around the docks and watch the gulls compete for handouts above the rusted shrimp boats. But do it soon: there's talk of a major condo development in the works that will likely put this sleepy port on the snowbird map. *15 mi east of St. George Island on U.S. 98.*

LITTLE ST. GEORGE ISLAND ◆ All that Little St. George can offer is a seemingly endless stretch of deserted beach and a lighthouse, which is slowly sliding into the sea. Camping is allowed by special permit. You'll need to take a charter boat out of Apalachicola to get here.

SHOP

Two Gulls (W. Pine Ave., tel. 850/927–2044) is one of the island's nicer shops, with beach-theme gifts and objets d'art.

OUTDOORS

Fishing is one of the main reasons people come here. Locals brag that in winter you can bag huge redfish in minutes right off the beach. Other local catches include sheepshead, mackerel, and cobia. Best spots include Bob Sikes Cut at the eastern point of St. George Island State Park. **Bay City Lodge** (1000 Bay City Rd., Apalachicola, tel. 850/653–9294, fax 850/653–8306, www.baycitylodge.com) offers charter fishing trips. **Fisherman's Headquarters** (40 W. Bayshore Dr., tel. 850/927–9817) sells bait, tackle, and fishing licenses, and rents rods and reels.

You can find boat ramps at St. George Island State Park at the youth camp and east slough areas. For a boat tour of St. George Sound and Apalachicola Bay, call charter captain **A. P. Whaley** (Box 696, Carrabelle 32322, tel. 850/697–3989). He's famous in these parts for his uncanny ability to attract dolphin to the stern of his boat, the *Gat V.*

Jeanni's Journeys (240 E. 3rd St., tel. 850/927–3259, fax 850/927–3831, www.sgislandjourneys.com) is a sailing school that also offers canoeing, sightseeing and photographic cruises, and children's environmental excursions.

You can rent bicycles at **Fisherman's Headquarters** (40 W. Bayshore Dr., tel. 850/927–9817).

AFTER DARK

Don't come to St. George looking for swinging night scenes and cultural overload. On the island, there's only one place known for its nightlife. **Harry A's** (10 Bayshore Dr., tel. 850/927–9810) is a neighborhood bar with a big-screen TV, a pool table, and live country and rock bands.

EAT

BLUE PARROT ♦ You'll feel like you're sneaking in the back door as you climb the side stairs leading to an outdoor deck overlooking the gulf. Or if you can, grab a table indoors. During special-event weekends, the place is packed, and service may be a little slow. The food is hard to beat if you're not looking for anything fancy. Baskets of shrimp, oysters, and crab cakes—fried or chargrilled and served with fries—are more than one person can handle. Daily specials are on the blackboard. *$6–$22. 68 W. Gorrie Dr., tel. 850/927–2987, fax 850/927–3544. AE, D, MC, V.*

CARRABELLE JUNCTION ♦ Stop by this eclectic spot for a cup of gourmet coffee—no small feat in these parts—and freshly made classic sandwiches ranging from tuna salad to BLTs. Or get a scoop of ice cream, grab a table out front, and enjoy the music that Ron, the proprietor, spins on a real record player. Locally produced artwork and knickknacks are sold here, too. *$4–$6. 88 Tallahassee St., Carrabelle 32322, tel. 850/697–9550. No credit cards. No dinner.*

OYSTER COVE SEAFOOD BAR & GRILL ♦ Come here for a Florida menu—fresh fish, shrimp, oysters, etc.—alive with the spices and flavor of the Caribbean. The view can't be beat, either, since the place overlooks one of the finest beaches in the country. *$15–$25. 2000 Gun St., 32328, tel. 850/927–2600. AE, MC, V.*

SLEEP

More than 750 homes on St. George Island are for rent. The modest ones run about $400 a week. Grand, beachfront homes in St. George Plantation fetch up to $3,000. In season and over holidays, a one-week minimum stay is required. Rates are highest from May to September. **Anchor Vacation Realty** (119 Franklin Blvd., tel. 800/824–0416, fax 850/653–1510) handles house rentals. **Prudential Resort Realty** (118–120 Gulf Beach Dr. W, tel. 904/927–2666 or 800/332–5196) rents houses.

There are 60 campsites—available by reservation—at **St. George Island State Park** (tel. 850/927–2111 or 800/326–3521 reservations, www.reserveamerica.com).

THE ST. GEORGE INN ♦ A little piece of Key West smack in the middle of the Panhandle, this cozy inn has tin roofs, hardwood floors, wraparound porches—even a widow's walk. Personal touches like private porches and in-room coffeemakers keep things homey. Both beach and bay are within view, and several restaurants and a convenience store are within walking distance. Two larger suites have full kitchens, and the pool is heated for year-round swimming. Specials are posted on the inn's Web site during off-season, when prices can drop by more than half. *$79–$99, suites $159. 135 Franklin Blvd., 32320, tel. 800/332–5196 (press 1) reservations or 850/927–2903, www.stgeorgeinn.com. 15 rooms; 2 suites. Some kitchens, refrigerators, cable TV, pool. MC, V.*

MORE INFO

APALACHICOLA BAY CHAMBER OF COMMERCE ♦ *122 Commerce St., Apalachicola 32320, tel. 850/653–9419, fax 850/653–8219, www. apalachicolabay.org.*

GETTING HERE

From Tallahassee Regional Airport (two hours from the island), turn right on Capital Circle SW (Route 263) and continue about 3½ mi. Turn right (south) on U.S. 319, and drive 32 mi to where it merges with U.S. 98 in Medart. Continue south on U.S. 98 to Ochlockonee Bay, then west to Eastpoint (another 30 mi). In Eastpoint, turn left on Island Drive (watch for signs to St. George Island) and continue across Franklin Bridge to the island.

TALLAHASSEE

I–10 rolls east over the timid beginnings of the Appalachian foothills and through thick pines into the state capital, with its canopies of ancient oaks and spring bowers of azaleas. Along with Florida State University, the perennial Seminoles football champions, and FAMU's fabled "Marching 100" band, the city also has more than a touch of the Old South. Tallahassee maintains a tranquillity quite different from the sun-and-surf hedonism of the major coastal towns. Acknowledging the cosmopolitan pace of other Florida cities, residents claim their hometown is "Florida with a southern accent." Vestiges of the city's colorful past are found throughout; for example, in the capitol complex, the turn-of-the-20th-century Old Capitol building is strikingly paired with the New Capitol skyscraper. Tallahassee's tree-lined streets are particularly memorable—among the best canopied roads are St. Augustine, Miccosukee, Meridian, Old Bainbridge, and Centerville, all dotted with country stores and antebellum plantation houses.

SEE & DO

✪ **ALFRED MACLAY GARDENS STATE PARK** Starting in December the grounds are afire with azaleas, dogwood, and other showy or rare plants. Allow half a day to wander past the reflecting pool into the tiny walled garden, and around the lakes and woodlands. The Maclay residence, furnished as it was in the 1920s; picnic areas; and swimming and boating facilities are open to the public. The gardens are both peaceful and perfect. *3540 Thomasville Rd., 32309, tel. 850/487–4556, www.ssnow.com/maclay. Jan.–Apr. $6.25 per vehicle, up to 8 people; May–Dec. $4. Daily 8 AM–dusk.*

APALACHICOLA NATIONAL FOREST ♦ The state's largest forest, with 564,000 acres, is full of rivers, creeks, lakes, sink holes, and savannahs—excellent habitats for rare and endangered plants and animals. The forest, which has several interpretive hiking trails, extends west from 30 mi southwest of Tallahassee to the Apalachicola River. U.S. 319 at Sopchoppy is a main entrance to the forest. To get to the closest forest service office, take Highway 20 south to Bristol, about a 45-minute drive. *11152 NW S.R. 20, Bristol 32321, tel. 850/643–2282, www.southernregion.fs.fed.us/florida. Free. Daily 8 AM–dusk.*

✪ DOWNTOWN TALLAHASSEE HISTORIC TRAIL A route originally mapped and documented by an eager Eagle Scout as part of a merit-badge project, this trail has become a Tallahassee sightseeing staple. The starting point is the New Capitol, where at the visitor center you can pick up maps and descriptive brochures. You can walk through the **Park Avenue and Calhoun Street historic districts,** which will take you back to Territorial days and the era of postwar reconstruction. The trail is dotted with landmark churches and cemeteries, along with outstanding examples of Greek revival, Italianate, and Prairie-style architecture. Some houses are open to the public. The **Brokaw-McDougall House** (329 N. Meridian St., weekdays 9–3, free) is a superb example of the Greek revival and Italianate styles. The **Meginnis-Monroe House** (125 N. Gadsden St., Tues.–Sat. 10–5, Sun. 2–5, free) served as a field hospital during the Civil War and is now an art gallery.

✪ **EDWARD BALL WAKULLA SPRINGS STATE PARK** One of the world's largest and deepest sweetwater springs is a highlight of this 2,860-acre park, which is 15 mi south of Tallahassee on Route 61. Famed explorer Ponce de León thought these springs were his long sought-after "fountain of youth" when he discovered them in 1513. The park retains the wild and junglelike beauty it had in the 1930s, when *Tarzan* movies were filmed here. You can have a picnic and hike on 6 mi of trails. There are daily boat tours. *550 Wakulla Park Dr., Wakulla Springs, tel. 850/922–3632, www. floridastateparks.org/wakullasprings. $4 per vehicle. Daily 8–dusk.*

FLORIDA AGRICULTURAL AND MECHANICAL UNIVERSITY ◆ One of the three oldest schools in the Florida State University system, this land grant university was founded in 1887. On Florida A&M's 419 rolling acres you'll find the Lee Hall Auditorium, a performing arts center, and the Black Archives Research Center and Museum, among other structures. *Martin Luther King Blvd. and Wahnish Way, 32307, tel. 850/599–3000 or 850/599–3020, www. famu.edu. Free. Tours Mon.–Thurs. at 9, 11, and 2; Fri. at 9 and 11.*

BLACK ARCHIVES RESEARCH CENTER AND MUSEUM ◆ Oral history tapes, manuscripts, art works, photographs, and artifacts document the history and culture of Africans and African-Americans at this archive and museum. The complex is in the university's 1907 Carnegie Library. *Gamble St. and Martin Luther King Blvd., tel. 850/599–3020. Free. Weekdays 9–4.*

FLORIDA STATE UNIVERSITY ◆ The university's School of Music regularly hosts concerts and recitals, performances by the Tallahassee Symphony Orchestra, and a number of productions by its top-rated theater program. *132 N. Copeland St., tel. 850/644–4774, 850/644–3246 tour reservations, www.fsu.edu. Free. Campus open daily; walking and driving tours weekdays during school year.*

GOVERNOR'S MANSION ◆ The residence of Florida's chief executive is a Georgian-style Southern mansion styled after President Andrew Jackson's Hermitage. A one-hour tour highlights the home's collection of French impressionist paintings, antique furnishings, and gifts from foreign dignitaries. *700 N. Adams St., 32303, tel. 850/488–4661. Free. Mar.–May, daily 10–noon.*

LAKE JACKSON MOUNDS ARCHAEOLOGICAL STATE PARK ♦ Here are waters to make bass anglers weep. For sightseers, Indian mounds and the ruins of an early-19th-century plantation built by Colonel Robert Butler, adjutant to General Andrew Jackson during the siege of New Orleans, are found along the shores of the lake. *3600 Indian Mounds Rd., tel. 850/562–0042. $2. Daily 8 AM–dusk.*

LEMOYNE ART FOUNDATION ♦ Once a field hospital during the Civil War, the historic Meginnis–Monroe House now holds rotating shows—from student artwork to local and national artists. The permanent collection is diverse and includes a tranquil sculpture garden. Educational art programs are held weekly as well. *125 Gadsden St., 32301, tel. 850/222–8800, www.lemoyne.org. $1. Tues.–Sat. 10–5, Sun. 1–5. Closed Nov. 1–Thanksgiving.*

MACLAY STATE GARDENS ♦ New York financier Alfred B. Maclay created a masterpiece of garden design on the rolling hills overlooking Lake Hall, some 5½ mi north of Tallahassee via U.S. 319. Maclay began developing the property in 1923 as his family's southern retreat. In spring the grounds are abloom with azaleas, dogwood, and other flowers. You can have a picnic, or, in Lake Hall, go swimming, boating, or fishing for largemouth bass, bream, and bluegill. *3540 Thomasville Rd., tel. 850/487–4556, www.ssnow. com/maclay. $4 per vehicle. Park daily 8 AM–dusk; gardens daily 9–5.*

MISSION SAN LUIS ♦ This museum focuses on the archaeology of 17th-century Spanish mission and Apalachee Indian town sites. In its heyday, in 1675, the Apalachee village here had a population of at least 1,400. Threatened by Creek Indians and British forces in 1704, the locals burned the village and fled. Take self-guided tours and watch scientists conducting digs daily (usually). The museum's popular "Living History" program is held on the third Saturday of the month (10 AM–2 PM). *2020 W. Mission Rd., 32304, tel. 850/487–3711. Free. Tues.–Sun 10–4.*

✪ **MUSEUM OF FLORIDA HISTORY** If you thought Florida was founded by Walt Disney, stop here. Covering 12,000 years, the displays explain Florida's past by highlighting the unique geological and historical events that have shaped the state. Exhibits include a mammoth armadillo grazing in a savannah, the remains of a giant mastodon found in nearby Wakulla Springs, and a dugout canoe that once carried Indians into Florida's backwaters. *500 S. Bronough St., 32399, tel. 850/245–6400. dhr.dos.state.fl.us/museum. Free. Weekdays 9–4:30, Sat. 10–4:30, Sun. noon–4:30.*

NATURAL BRIDGE STATE HISTORIC SITE ♦ The site commemorates the Battle of Natural Bridge, which took place here on March 6, 1865. The battle in which Confederates prevented Union troops from capturing Tallahassee is reenacted every year in March. During the weekend reenactment you can view Confederate and Union encampments. *7502 Natural Bridge Rd., Woodville 32311, tel. 850/922–6007, www.floridastateparks.org. Free. Daily 8 AM–dusk.*

NEW CAPITOL ♦ This modern skyscraper looms up 22 stories directly behind the low-rise Old Capitol. From the fabulous 22nd-floor observation deck, on a clear day, catch a panoramic view of Tallahassee and the surrounding countryside—all the way into Georgia. Also on this floor is the Florida Artists Hall of Fame, a tribute to Floridians such as Ray Charles, Burt Reynolds, Tennessee Williams, Ernest Hemingway, and Marjorie Kinnan Rawlings. To pick up information about the area, stop at the Florida Visitors Center, on the plaza level. *400 S. Monroe St., tel. 850/488–6167. Free. Visitor center weekdays 8–5; self-guided or guided tours weekdays 8–5.*

OLD CAPITOL ♦ The centerpiece of the capitol complex, this pre–Civil War structure has been added to and subtracted from several times. Having been restored, the jaunty red-and-white stripe awnings and combination gas-electric lights make it look much as it did in 1902. Inside, historically accurate legislative chambers and exhibits offer a peek into the past. *400 S. Monroe St., 32301, tel. 850/487–1902. Free. Self-guided or guided tours weekdays 9–4:30, Sat. 10–4:30, Sun. noon–4:30.*

✪ ST. MARKS NATIONAL WILDLIFE REFUGE The salt marshes, hardwood swamps, pine flatwoods, and pine and oak uplands bordering Apalachee Bay make up this 64,934-acre refuge, which is 25 mi south of Tallahassee, via Route 363. Diked impoundments attract wintering waterfowl. There are 75 mi of trails for hiking, and you can bicycle on the refuge roads. Fort San Marcos de Apalachee was built here in 1639, and stones salvaged from the fort were used in the lighthouse, which is still in operation. On the beach and pilings nearby look for shorebirds, gulls, and terns. The visitor center has a small retail shop. *1255 Lighthouse Rd., St. Marks 32355, tel. 850/925–6121, fax 850/925–6930, saintmarks.fws.gov. $4 per vehicle, $1 per bicycle. Daily dawn–dusk; visitor center weekdays 8–4:15, weekends 10–5.*

☾ TALLAHASSEE MUSEUM OF HISTORY AND NATURAL SCIENCE ♦ It could have been dull, but this bucolic park showcases a peaceful and intriguing look at Old Florida. A working 1880s pioneer farm offers daily hands-on activities for children, such as soap making and blacksmithing. A boardwalk meanders through the 52 acres of natural habitat that make up the zoo, which has such varied animals as panthers, bobcats, white-tailed deer, and black bears. Also on site are nature trails, a one-room schoolhouse dating from 1897, and an 1840s southern plantation manor, where you can usually find someone cooking on the weekends. *3945 Museum Dr., tel. 850/576–1636, www.tallahasseemuseum. org. $7. Mon.–Sat. 9–5, Sun. 12:30–5.*

UNION BANK BUILDING ♦ Chartered in 1833, this is Florida's oldest bank building. Since it closed in 1843, it has played many roles, from ballet school to bakery. It has been restored to what is thought to be its original appearance and currently houses Florida A&M's Black Archives Extension, which depicts African-American history in Florida. Call ahead for hours, which are subject to change, and directions. *219 Apalachee Pkwy., 32301, tel. 850/487–3803. Free. Weekdays 9–4.*

AFTER DARK

Florida State University (tel. 850/644–4774 School of Music, 850/644–6500 School of Theatre, www.music.fsu.edu) annually hosts more than 400 concerts and recitals given year-round by its School of Music, and many productions by its School of Theatre. The **Monticello Opera House** (158 W. Washington St., Monticello 32344, tel. 850/997–4242) presents concerts and plays in a restored 1890s gaslight-era opera house. The **Tallahassee Little Theatre** (1861 Thomasville Rd., tel. 850/224–8474, www.tallytown.com/tlt) has a five-production season that runs from September through May. The season of the **Tallahassee Symphony Orchestra** (tel. 850/224–0461, www.tsolive.org) runs from October through April; performances are usually held at Florida State University's Ruby Diamond Auditorium.

Floyd's Music Store (666–1 W. Tennessee St., 32304, tel. 850/222–3506) hosts some of the hottest local and touring acts around. Other performers, from dueling pianos to Dave Matthews cover bands to assorted DJs, round out the schedule. Don't let the name fool you: the **Late Night Library** (809 Gay St., 32304, tel. 850/224–2429) is the quintessential college-town party bar. Think dancing, drinking, and you'll get the picture. **Waterworks** (1133 Thomasville Rd., 32303, tel. 850/224–1887), with its retro-chic tiki-bar fittings, attracts jazz fans and hipsters of all ages for live music and cocktails. Call for the latest on who's playing.

EAT

ALBERT'S PROVENCE ♦ Garden and other outdoor seating, an extensive wine list, and an eclectic menu distinguish this place. On the menu is mainly fresh local seafood, such as the red snapper Marseillaise (stuffed with crabmeat, baked with chablis, sour cream, and saffron, and topped with lobster sauce). On the meaty side is the roasted leg and rack of lamb Provençale, served with garlic mashed potatoes, fresh sautéed vegetables, and flageolet beans. *$13–$49. 1415 Timberlane Rd., in Market Sq., 32312, tel. 850/ 894–9003, www.albertsprovence.com. AE, D, MC, V. Closed Sun. No lunch Sat.*

✪ ANDREW'S 228 Part of a smart complex in the heart of the political district, this place serves classic food in a casual bistro style. For dinner, the tournedos St. Laurent and the peppered New York strip are both flawless. Seafood lovers can feast on the day's fresh catch. *$15–$25. 228 S. Adams St., 32301, tel. 850/222–3444, www. andrewsdowntown.com. AE, D, MC, V.*

BAHN THAI ♦ The simple dining area, with pale gold walls and brick archways between seating areas, creates a warm mood. The streetside buffet includes tasty pan-Asian dishes including coconut-milk soup and minced avocado salad. The menu includes such favorites as beef with snow peas and shrimp with golden rice. Bahn Thai also stocks a number of Asian beers and wines. *$10–$19. 1319 S. Monroe St., 32301, tel. 850/224–4765. AE, DC, MC, V. Closed Sun. No lunch Sat.*

BANJO'S SMOKEHOUSE ♦ Savory, slow-cooked meat covered with thick barbecue sauce is the specialty here, though you can also get chicken, pork, and beef. The baby back ribs and the USDA prime Black Angus steaks are popular. The dining area is cavernous and woody and accented with down-home knick-knacks. This place opens at 11 for lunch but closes relatively early (at 9 Sunday through Thursday and at 10 on Friday and Saturday). *$6–$17. 2335 Apalachee Pkwy., 32302, tel. 850/877–8111. Reservations not accepted. DC, MC, V. Closed Labor Day.*

BARNACLE BILL'S ♦ This casual restaurant has a gigantic menu with fresh seafood of all descriptions. Entrées come with fresh veggies on the side. This is a popular local hangout and can get a little loud at peak times. Children eat free on Sunday. *$6–$20. 1830 N. Monroe St., 32302, tel. 850/385–8734. Reservations not accepted. AE, DC, MC, V.*

CHEZ PIERRE ♦ You'll feel as if you've entered a great-aunt's old plantation home in this restored 1920s house set back from the road in historic Lafayette Park. Since 1876, its warm, cozy rooms, gleaming hardwood floors, and large French doors separating dining areas have created an intimate place to go for authentic French cuisine. Try the tournedos of beef or one of the special lamb dishes. *$6–$26. 1215 Thomasville Rd., 32303, tel. 850/222–0936, www.chezpierre.com. AE, D, DC, MC, V.*

✪ HOPKINS' EATERY Locals in the know flock here for superb salads, homemade soups, and sandwiches (so expect a short wait at lunchtime) via simple counter service. For kids there's the traditional PBJ sandwich; you may prefer the chunky chicken melt, smothered beef, or garden vegetarian sub. The orange-and-spearmint iced tea is delicious, as is the freshly baked chocolate cake. A second location on North Monroe Street serves lunch only. *$4–$7. 1415 Market St., 32312, tel. 850/668–0311; 1840 N. Monroe St., tel. 850/386–4258. AE, D, DC, MC, V. Closed Sun. No dinner Sat.*

KOOL BEANZ CAFÉ ♦ In the heart of downtown Tallahasee is this trendy spot where the menu changes nightly. You can expect seafood, meat, pasta, and vegetarian dishes. The space is small, centered on the open kitchen and bar area, and on the walls are bright, modern art. *$8–$18. 921 Thomasville Rd., 32303, tel. 850/224–2466, fax 850/224–1233. AE, D, MC, V. Closed Sun. No lunch Sat.*

LONGHORN STEAKS ♦ This casual steak house just across the street from the Tallahasee Mall is a good place to rest your feet at the shotgun-style bar or a large wooden table. "Cowboy"-style fare means a lot of beef, all cut fresh in house. If you want something lighter, try the grilled salmon marinated in Bourbon sauce. *$9–$20. 2400 N. Monroe St., 32303, tel. 850/385–4028, fax 850/ 383–0466. AE, D, DC, MC, V.*

THE MELTING POT ♦ The booths have high backs for privacy, and the candlelight makes for romantic fondue dipping. You cook most dishes over a flame and dip them in your chosen sauce. The "French Quarter" meal comes with andouille sausage, shrimp, beef tenderloin, and chicken, plus a variety of sauces, such as Gorgonzola-port or lemon-pepper. For dessert you can get a platter of fruit and cakes—to be dipped in chocolaty amaretto or Bailey's Irish Cream sauce. *$12–$30. 2727 N. Monroe St., 32303, tel. 850/ 386–7440, fax 850/386–8410, www.meltingpot.com. AE, D, DC, MC, V. No lunch.*

MONROE ST. GRILLE ♦ This restaurant in a Ramada Inn is casual yet polished. The Grille's claim to fame is its 100-item salad bar, which includes everything from garbanzo beans to chocolate mousse. The menu includes prime rib, steaks, and seafood selections. It's open for breakfast, too. *$8–$17. 2700 N. Monroe St., 32301, tel. 850/386–1027. Reservations not accepted. AE, D, DC, MC, V.*

MORI JAPANESE STEAKHOUSE ♦ Bamboo plants and watercolors on the wooden walls evoke Japan. Try steaks, sushi, or hibachi (for which a chef prepares your meal table-side). *$12–$25. 2810 Charer Rd., 32312, tel. 850/386–7653. AE, MC, V. No lunch.*

NICHOLSON'S FARMHOUSE ♦ The name says a lot about this friendly, informal country place with an outside kitchen and grill. A few miles out in the Tallahassee countryside, the steak house is a retreat from the already calming capital city. A farm, gift shop, mule-drawn wagon rides, and a folk guitarist named Hoot Gibson (not the astronaut) create a rural retreat where you can enjoy hand-cut steaks, chops, and seafood. *$11–$32. From U.S. 27 follow Rte. 12 toward Quincy and look for signs, tel. 850/539–5931, fax 850/ 539–1338, www.nicholsonfarmhouse.com. AE, D, MC, V. BYOB. Closed Sun. and Mon. No lunch.*

NINO ♦ You can dine outdoors on the big front deck at this restaurant surrounded by trees. The *scampi all'aglio* is a handful of jumbo shrimp lightly dredged in flour then sautéed in olive oil with lemon, white wine, and garlic. *$9–$20. 6497 Apalachee Pkwy., 32301, tel. 850/878–8141. AE, D, DC, MC, V. Closed Sun. and Mon. No lunch.*

ON THE BORDER ♦ Saddles and bull's heads give this place a cowboy vibe. Dine indoors or out on the covered patio, or sip your margaritas at the bar (draft beer and margaritas are always 2 for 1). The house specialty is the Ultimate Fajitas, which includes steak, chicken, ribs, shrimp, and roasted red potatoes on a sizzling platter. The pico shrimp and chicken dish is topped with a spicy pico de gallo sauce and melted jack cheese. *$8–$13. 1650 N. Monroe St., 32303, tel. 850/521–9887, www.ontheborder.com. AE, D, MC, V.*

✪ RICE-BOWL ORIENTAL Bamboo woodwork and thatched-roof booths lend an air of authenticity to this Asian-hybrid spot tucked away in a Tallahassee strip mall. Chinese, Japanese, Thai, and Vietnamese favorites are all represented here, from General Tso's Chicken to fresh sushi to green curry and rice noodle dishes. The all-you-can-eat lunch buffet (Sunday through Friday 11:30–2) is only $6.60. $7–$15. 3813 N. Monroe St., tel. 850/514–3632. AE, D, DC, MC, V.

SAMRAT ♦ Occupying a former fast-food joint, this place is nothing fancy. But the chefs turn out good tandoori chicken (chicken cooked in a tandoor, or clay, oven with mild Indian spices). The *paneer masala* consists of homemade cheese tossed in butter and cultured yogurt and served with creamy sauce and rice. $9–$19. 2529 Apalachee Pkwy., tel. 850/942–1993. AE, DC, MC, V. Closed weekdays 2:30–5.

SILVER SLIPPER ♦ A number of U.S. presidents, including John F. Kennedy and George Bush, have enjoyed this hallowed establishment founded in 1938, and certainly this place caters to a largely political clientele. There's a crystal chandelier in the lobby. Curtained booths for two are off the main dining area. The 2-inch-thick filet mignon practically melts under its crispy charred crust. There's a large wine list. Desserts include white chocolate mousse cake. $14–$35. 531 Silver Slipper La., 32301, tel. 850/386–9366, www.thesilverslipper.com. AE, D, DC, MC, V. Closed Sun. No lunch.

SLEEP

CABOT LODGE-NORTH ♦ This motel on 6 quiet acres feels more like a B&B or a resort lodge than a motel. The huge, wraparound porch overlooks shaded grounds and walking paths. Rooms have homey attractiveness, with antique reproduction furnishings and wooden beds. $72–$78. 2735 N. Monroe St., 32304, tel. 850/386–8880, 800/223–1964 reservations, fax 850/386–4254, www.cabotlodge.com. 160 rooms. Complimentary Continental breakfast, cable TV, pool, laundry facilities, business services. AE, D, MC, V.

CABOT LODGE, THOMASVILLE RD ♦ This stately five-story, pale-vanilla stucco building sits on a little rise amid pruned evergreen shrubbery. Rooms are somewhat stark, with almost-bare white walls and dark carpet. All have generous work spaces and upholstered lounge chairs. *$74–$91, $122 on football weekends. 1653 Raymond Diehl Rd., 32308, tel. 850/386–7500, 800/223–1964 reservations, fax 850/386–1136, www.cabotlodgethomasvilleroad.com. 135 rooms. Complimentary Continental breakfast, in-room data ports, cable TV, in-room VCRs with movies, pool, laundry facilities, business services. AE, D, MC, V.*

COMFORT INN ♦ Rooms at this three-story, green-and-white motel have deep ochre and sage hues. Sleeping areas are separated from sitting areas by high arched doorways. The motel is 1 mi from the Capitol and within 5 mi of most museums and galleries. *$62–$87. 2727 Graves Rd., 32303, tel. 850/562–7200, fax 850/562–6335, www.choicehotels.com/stay/florida. 100 rooms. In-room data ports, microwaves, refrigerators, pool, laundry facilities. AE, D, MC, V.*

COMFORT SUITES ♦ This three-story all-suites hotel is ½ mi from the Capitol and less than 2 mi from Florida State University and Florida A&M University. Rooms are done in earth tones; some have whirlpool tubs. *$89–$99. 1026 Apalachee Pkwy., 32301, tel. 850/224–3200 or 888/224–1254, fax 850/224–2206, www.choicehotels.com. 64 suites. Complimentary Continental breakfast, in-room data ports, in-room safes, microwaves, refrigerators, cable TV, exercise equipment, business services. AE, D, DC, MC, V.*

COURTYARD BY MARRIOTT ♦ This four-story property 2 mi from Florida A&M and Florida State and 1 mi from the Capitol is on Tallahassee's motel strip. Rooms have large, well-lit work spaces and sitting areas. *$89–99; $149 suites. 1018 Apalachee Pkwy., 32301, tel. 850/222–8822, 800/443–6000 reservations, fax 850/561–*

0354, www.marriott.com. 141 rooms; 13 suites. Restaurant, in-room data ports, refrigerators, cable TV, pool, exercise equipment, hot tub, bar, laundry facilities, business services. AE, D, MC, V.

DOUBLETREE HOTEL TALLAHASSEE ♦ This hotel a mere two blocks from the capitol hosts heavy hitters from the worlds of politics and media. Since it's also an easy walk from the Florida State University campus, it welcomes plenty of FSU fans during football season. Rooms are basic and have two full-size beds—these are pushed together to create a "king" bed. *$109–$129, $179 on football weekends. 101 S. Adams St., 32301, tel. 850/224–5000, fax 850/513–9516, www.hiltonhotel.com. 243 rooms. Restaurant, cable TV, pool, gym, bar. AE, D, DC, MC, V.*

✪ EDWARD BALL WAKULLA SPRINGS LODGE AND CONFERENCE CENTER This lodge, about an hour's drive south of downtown Tallahassee, was completed in 1937, and most of the rooms reflect this era. Furnishings are simple, and there's a large fireplace in the lobby. You can hike in the surrounding Wakulla Park and swim year-round in 70-degree Wakulla Springs. Or take an educational or sightseeing tour ($25 per person) on a glass-bottom boat. *$79 weekdays, $99 weekends. 550 Wakulla Park Dr., Wakulla Springs 32305, tel. 850/224–5950, fax 850/561–7251, www.wakullacounty.com/wakulla-24.htm. 27 rooms. Restaurant, playground; no room TVs. MC, V.*

✪ GOVERNORS INN Only a block from the capitol, this plushly restored warehouse is abuzz during the week with politicians, press, and lobbyists. It's a perfect location for business travelers and on weekends for tourists who want to visit downtown sites. Rooms are a rich blend of mahogany, brass, and classic prints. The VIP treatment includes cocktails and a daily paper. *$159 rooms, $169–$229 suites. 209 S. Adams St., 32301, tel. 850/681–6855, 800/342–7717 in Florida, fax 850/222–3105, www.thegovinn.com. 28 rooms; 12 suites. Cable TV, laundry service. AE, D, DC, MC, V. CP.*

HAMPTON INN ♦ Rooms are basic at this frill-free motel, which also offers handicap accessible rooms and is north of downtown off I–10. *$99; $139 suite. 3210 N. Monroe St., 32303, tel. 850/562–4300, fax 850/562–6735, www.hamptoninn.com. 95 rooms; 1 suite. In-room data ports, microwaves, refrigerators, cable TV, pool, laundry facilities, business services. AE, D, MC, V.*

HILTON GARDEN INN TALLAHASSEE ♦ Wrapped around a palm-shaded pool area, this four-story lodging has a comfortable lounge with a view of swimmers and sunbathers outside. Rooms are done in a breezy, tropical style with lots of pale colors and airbrushed wall art. *$74–$129. 3333 Thomasville Rd., 32308, tel. 850/385–3553 or 800/916–2221, fax 850/385–4242, www.hilton.com. 100 rooms. Restaurant, in-room data ports, microwaves, refrigerators, cable TV, pool, exercise equipment, hot tub, bar, laundry facilities, business services. AE, D, MC, V.*

HOLIDAY INN SELECT DOWNTOWN ♦ This hotel is a few blocks from the Capitol and within a 2-mi radius of Florida State University and Florida A&M University. *$160; $180 suites. 316 W. Tennessee St., 32301, tel. 850/222–9555 or 800/648–6135, fax 850/224–8410, www.holiday-inn.com. 164 rooms; 11 suites. Restaurant, room service, in-room data ports, pool, gym, laundry facilities, concierge, business services, airport shuttle. AE, D, DC, MC, V.*

HOLIDAY INN, NORTHWEST ♦ This two-story hotel has a covered drive and pale stucco exterior. Rooms are done in dark pine greens and earthy browns. It's within walking distance of shops and restaurants and 5 mi from the Governor's Square Mall. *$66–$89. 2714 Graves Rd., 32303, tel. 850/562–2000 or 800/465–4329, fax 850/562–8519, www.holiday-inn.com. 179 rooms. Restaurant, in-room data ports, microwaves, refrigerators, cable TV, pool, bar, laundry facilities, business services, some pets allowed, no-smoking rooms. AE, D, MC, V.*

HOWARD JOHNSON EXPRESS INN ♦ This chain property is 3 mi north of the Capitol and ½ mi south of the Tallahassee Mall. Some of the rooms face the pool. *$65. 2726 N. Monroe St., 32303, tel. 850/386–5000 or 800/406–1411, fax 850/386–5000, www.hojo. com. 52 rooms. Complimentary Continental breakfast, cable TV, pool, business services, no-smoking rooms. AE, D, DC, MC, V.*

MICROTEL INN & SUITES ♦ This motel 20 minutes from downtown caters mainly to a business crowd. *$61, $75 suites, $150 suites on football weekends. 3216 N. Monroe St., 32303, tel. 850/562–3800 or 888/771–7171, fax 850/562–8611, www.microtelinn.com. 61 rooms; 20 suites. Complimentary Continental breakfast, gym. AE, D, DC, MC, V.*

QUALITY INN AND SUITES ♦ Three miles from both Florida A&M and Florida State, this is a good choice for those in town for a football game. Rooms are basic motel. The Governor's Square Mall is 1 mi away, the Capitol 2 mi. *$79–$89, $175 on football weekends, $120 suites ($200 suites during special-event weekends). 2020 Apalachee Pkwy., 32301, tel. 850/877–4437, fax 850/878–9964, www. qualityinn.com. 90 rooms, 9 suites. Complimentary Continental breakfast, in-room data ports, microwaves, refrigerators, cable TV, pool, exercise equipment, laundry facilities, business services, free parking. AE, D, MC, V.*

RADISSON HOTEL TALLAHASSEE ♦ The lobby of this stately, seven-story white masonry building is naturally illuminated during daylight hours by large bay windows looking out onto well-tended grounds. Rooms are large and furnished with antique reproductions in dark cherrywood veneer. *$79–$159; $169–$199 suites. 415 N. Monroe St., 32301, tel. 850/224–6000, fax 850/224–6000, www.radisson.com. 112 rooms; 7 suites. Restaurant, in-room data ports, some in-room hot tubs, refrigerators, cable TV, in-room VCRs with movies, exercise equipment, bar, laundry facilities, business services, airport shuttle, free parking. AE, D, MC, V.*

RAMADA INN, NORTH ♦ Situated on 13 acres of landscaped grounds, this motel has a pleasant lobby with high ceilings. Rooms are done in mauve. *$119–$129, $149 suites. 2900 N. Monroe St., 32303, tel. 850/386–1027, fax 850/422–1025, www.ramada.com. 200 rooms. Restaurant, microwaves, refrigerators, cable TV, in-room VCRs with movies, pool, bar, business services, airport shuttle, free parking, some pets allowed. AE, D, MC, V.*

SHONEY'S INN ♦ The quiet courtyard with its own pool and the welcoming cantina convey the look of Old Spain. Rooms are furnished in heavy Mediterranean style—but only have double beds. Rates jump $30 on game weekends. *$59 doubles, $79 town houses, $154 Jacuzzi suites. 2801 N. Monroe St., 32303, tel. 850/386–8286, fax 850/422–1074, www.shoneysinn.com. 113 rooms; 25 town houses; 2 Jacuzzi suites. Complimentary Continental breakfast, some microwaves, some refrigerators, cable TV, pool, meeting rooms. AE, D, DC, MC, V.*

TOWNEPLACE SUITES MARRIOTT ♦ These roomy town house–style Marriott suites come in studio, one-bedroom, and two-bedroom varieties. Rooms are beige with green carpet. The hotel is 5 mi from the Capitol and the Tallahassee Museum of History and Natural Science, and 20 mi from Wakulla Springs State Park. *$99–$119. 1876 Capital Circle NE, 32308, tel. 850/219–0122, fax 850/219–0133, www.marriott.com. 95 suites. Kitchens, cable TV, pool, gym, laundry facilities, business services, some pets allowed (fee).*

MORE INFO

TALLAHASSEE AREA CONVENTION AND VISITORS BUREAU ♦ (106 E. Jefferson St., Tallahassee 32301, tel. 850/413–9200 or 800/628–2866, www.seetallahassee.com).

GETTING HERE

Tallahassee is the largest city in the Florida Panhandle. I–10 cuts through Tallahassee from west to east, with the downtown area to the south of the interstate.

Tallahassee Regional Airport is served by AirTran, Atlantic Southeast–Delta, Delta, Delta Connection, Skywest, and US Airways Express. To get to Tallahassee from the airport, take State Road 263 east to State Road 319, known locally as Capitol Circle, which curves north and intersects with Apalachee Parkway. Turn left (west) on Apalachee Parkway, which dead-ends 3 mi later at the Old Capitol, downtown.

INDEX

Notes

Notes

Notes